CONTENTS

Introduction

Food Finder

Our choice:

INTRODUCTION

Time for Food guides are designed to help you find interesting and enjoyable places to eat in the world's main tourist destinations. Each guide divides the destination into eight areas. Each area has a map, followed by a selection of the restaurants, cafés, bars, pubs and food markets in that area. The aim is to cover the whole spectrum of food establishments, from gourmet temples to humble cafés, plus good food shops or delicatessens where you can buy picnic ingredients or food to cook yourself.

If you are looking for a particular restaurant, regardless of its location, or a particular type of cuisine, you can turn to the Food Finder, starting on page 4. This lists all the establishments reviewed in this guide

by name (in alphabetical order) and then by cuisine type.

PRICES

Unlike some guides, we have not wasted space telling you how bad a restaurant is – bad or poor-value restaurants simply do not make it into the guide. Many other guides ask restaurants to pay for their entries, or expect the restaurant to advertise in return for a listing. We do neither of these things: the restaurants and cafés featured here simply represent a selection of places that the authors have sampled and enjoyed.

If there is one consistent criterion for inclusion in the guide, it is good value. Good value does not, of course,

mean cheap necessarily. Food lovers know the difference between a restaurant where the high prices are fully justified by the quality of the ingredients and the excellence of the cooking and presentation of the food, and meretricious establishments where high prices are merely the result of pretentious attitudes.

Some of the restaurants featured here are undeniably expensive if you consume caviar and champagne, but a few haute cuisine establishments often offer equally high-quality food at lower prices at lunchtime, allowing budget diners to enjoy dishes created by top chefs and every bit as good as those on the evening menu. At the same time, some of the eating places listed here might not make it into more conventional food guides, because they are relatively humble cafés or takeaways. Some are deliberately oriented towards tourists, but there is nothing wrong in that: what some guides dismiss as 'tourist traps' may be deservedly popular for providing choice and good value.

FEEDBACK

You may or may not agree with the authors' choice – in either case we would like to know about your experiences. Any feedback you give us and any recommendations you make will be followed up, so that you can look forward to seeing your restaurant suggestions in print in the next edition.

Feedback forms have been included at the back of the book and you can e-mail us with comments by writing to: *timeforfood@thomascook.com*. No food guide can keep pace with the changing restaurant scene, as chefs move on, establishments open or close, and menus, opening hours or credit card details change. Let us know what you like or do not like about the restaurants featured here. Tell us if you discover shops, pubs, cafés, bars, restaurants or markets that

you think should go in the guide. Let us know if you discover changes – say to telephone numbers or opening times.

Symbols used in this guide

VISA	Visa accepted
◎	Diners Club accepted
MasterCard	MasterCard accepted
🍴	Restaurant
🍺	Bar, café or pub
🧺	Shop, market or picnic site
📞	Telephone
◎	Transport
②	Numbered red circles relate to the maps at the start of the section

The price indications used in this guide have the following meanings.

$	budget level
$$	typical/average for the destination
$$$	up-market

FOOD FINDER

Beacon Hill

One of Boston's most exclusive neighbourhoods, Beacon Hill has an eatery for everyone, from ultra-casual cafés to small bistros, to a few of the highest-priced and most chic dining rooms in the city. Most restaurants are found on the peripheral streets – Charles, Cambridge and Beacon – of this densely residential area.

BEACON HILL
Restaurants

75 Chestnut ❶

75 Chestnut St

✆ 617-227-2175

Ⓜ Subway to Charles/MGH

Open: dinner daily 1730–2200, Sun brunch 1200–1500

Reservations recommended

All credit cards accepted

New American

❸❺

Few travellers ever stumble across this cosy, stylish neighbourhood favourite. The cuisine favours American culinary school standards – eg, herb-crusted rack of lamb, pan-roasted scallops and mussels in Chardonnay cream sauce.

Antonio's Cucina Italiana ❷

288 Cambridge St

✆ 617-367-3310

Ⓜ Subway to Charles/MGH

Open: Mon–Thu 1100–2200, Fri–Sat 1100–2230, closed Sun

Reservations unnecessary

🅥🅲 American Express Discover

Italian

❺

The traditional southern Italian dishes in this humble little restaurant are surprisingly good, unusually inexpensive and served with genuine enthusiasm. Reservations aren't usually needed in order to savour the tasty lobster ravioli in tomato-cream sauce because hardened foodies consider this side of Beacon Hill to be decidedly *déclassé*.

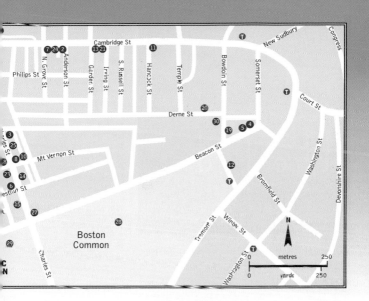

Artù

89 Charles St

⌀ 617-227-9023

🚇 Subway to Charles/MGH

Open: Mon–Sat 1100–2200,
Sun 1100–2100

Reservations recommended

💳 🅰 American Express

Italian

💲

You don't get much
elbowroom at the
cramped, low tables in
this semi-subterranean
eatery, but you don't
pay for elbowroom
either. Artù is known
for its marinated
roasted vegetables (in
theory an *antipasto*)
and its grilled lamb,
served either as thick
sandwiches or sliced on

a plate for dinner. Lunch is a steal.

Black Goose

21 Beacon St

∅ 617-720-4500

🚇 Subway to Park St

Open: Mon–Fri 1100–2200, Sat 1700–2400, Sun 1030–2200

Reservations recommended

💳 💳 American Express

Italian-New American

💲💲

With reasonably priced sandwiches and fresh salads for the midday State House and ad agency crowd, Black Goose metamorphoses into a semi-elegant Northern Italian dining room at night, with good cuts of tender beef and hearty pastas.

The Fed ❺

15 Beacon St

∅ 617-670-2515

🚇 Subway to Park St

Open: breakfast 0700–1030; lunch 1130–1430; dinner 1730–2230

Reservations essential

All credit cards accepted

New American-French

💲💲💲

Boston's arch temple of conspicuous consumption is feet away from the State House and big corporate law firms. Dollops of caviar are ubiquitous, but the nouveau French cooking beneath the glamour is solid. Well-heeled gourmands would do well to choose the 11-course tasting menu.

Figs ❻

42 Charles St

∅ 617-742-3447

🚇 Subway to Charles/MGH

Open: Mon–Fri 1730–2200, Sat 1200–2200, Sun 1200–2100

Reservations not allowed

💳 💳 American Express

Italian

💲

Figs is tops for grilled pizzas and pressed sandwiches, especially for weekend lunch. The hearty helpings of baked pasta dishes are legendary. If you really like the food, you can buy the cookbook or splurge at chef Todd English's fine-dining restaurant, **Olives**, in Charlestown (*see page 71*).

Harvard Gardens ❼

316 Cambridge St

∅ 617-523-2727

🚇 Subway to Charles/MGH

Open: Mon–Thu 1130–2300, Fri–Sat 1130–2400, closed Sun

Reservations unnecessary

💳 💳 American Express

Italian-American

💲

Harvard Gardens didn't need to change when 'Faux Fifties' became a look in Boston dining rooms – it already epitomised the style. An immense, smoky bar almost overwhelms the dining area, but the place is known for its retro steak tips as well as unusual pizzas, including some topped with artichoke hearts.

The Hungry i ❽

71 Charles St

∅ 617-227-3524

🚇 Subway to Charles/MGH

Open: Mon–Sun 1800–2130, Sun brunch 1100–1400

Reservations recommended

All credit cards accepted

French

🍷🍷🍷

Unrepentant classic French dishes are the strength at this warren of small rooms, and unapologetic French prices go with them. The Hungry i has a romantic reputation, especially among fans of pre-Truffaut Gallic films.

The King & I

145 Charles St

✆ 617-227-3320

🚇 Subway to Charles/MGH

Open: lunch Mon–Fri 1130–1645, Sat 1200–1645; dinner Mon–Thu, Sun 1700–2130, Fri–Sat 1700–2030

Reservations unnecessary

💳 💳 Discover

Thai-Vegetarian

🍷

Crisp, fresh vegetables find their way into every dish, and spice levels are unusually high for refined Beacon Hill tastes. Still, many locals favour this Thai

pioneer for quick suppers and takeaways.

Lala Rokh 🔟

97 Mt Vernon St

✆ 617-720-5511

🚇 Subway to Charles/MGH

Open: Mon–Sat 1730–2200

Reservations recommended

All credit cards accepted

Middle Eastern

🍷🍷

Persian cuisine was the mother of most North African cuisine and a lot of European fancy cooking, and here it's given an unusually serious treatment. The waiters will help decipher such exotic dishes as cold sautéed spinach puréed with yoghurt or the kebabs of Cornish game hen marinated in lemons and onions. Fancy a dessert? Try the stuffed dates in walnut paste.

Ma Soba 🔢

156 Cambridge St

✆ 617-973-6680

🚇 Subway to Charles/MGH

Open: Mon–Wed 1130–2230, Thu–Fri 1130–2300, Sat 1200–2300, Sun 1200–2230

Reservations recommended

All credit cards accepted

Oriental

🍷🍷

Skip the Asian fusion dishes, which are a confusing lot anyway, and concentrate on some of the best sushi in the city. If raw fish doesn't entice you, head straight for the Korean dishes, as they seem to best suit the creators in the kitchen.

No 9 Park 🔢

9 Park St

✆ 617-742-9991

🚇 Subway to Park St

Open: lunch Mon–Fri 1130–1430; dinner Mon–Sat 1730–2200; closed Sun

Reservations essential

All credit cards accepted

New American

🍷🍷🍷

Chef and co-owner Barbara Lynch is

something of a local culinary star as well as the darling of the national food media. She cooks with both gusto and finesse. Duck any way Lynch wants to cook it is always a good bet, and she transforms fish from duty into delight. Hobnob with local sports figures, politicians and dot.com whiz-kids at the bar.

Phoenicia

240 Cambridge St

∅ 617-523-4606

🚇 Subway to Charles/MGH

Open: Mon–Sat 1100–2300, Sun 1100–2200

Reservations unnecessary

All credit cards accepted

Middle Eastern

⑤

Practically across Cambridge St from Mass General Hospital, Phoenicia gets a lot of doctors and nurses dropping in for quick meals of Lebanese food. Sure, there are fast food places offering similar kebabs and stuffed eggplant (aubergine), but at Phoenicia you can sit down at a table with a tablecloth and order a glass of wine.

Ristorante Toscano ⑭

47 Charles St

∅ 617-723-4090

🚇 Subway to Charles/MGH

Open: lunch Mon–Sat 1130–1430; dinner daily 1730–2200

Reservations recommended

All credit cards accepted

Italian

⑤⑤⑤

In Beacon Hill's pioneer northern Italian restaurant, still going strong after many years, the menu, like the name, is solidly Tuscan. The strikingly good fresh pastas are available as main courses or as half servings as a first course. Roasted meats are the house speciality but daily fish dishes are usually superb.

Torch ⑮

26 Charles St

∅ 617-723-5939

🚇 Subway to Charles/MGH

Open: Tue–Thu, Sun 1700–2200, Fri–Sat 1700–2230

Reservations recommended

All credit cards accepted

French

⑤⑤

Chef-owner Evan Deluty trained and worked in Parisian bistros, and he's brought the look, taste and feel to Beacon Hill with a fine hangar steak and great sliced duck breast. For dessert, choose the intense cheeses.

BEACON HILL
Bars, cafés and pubs

21st Amendment ⑲

148 Bowdoin St

Ⓣ Subway to Park St

Open: Mon–Fri 1030–0200,
Sat 1200–0200

All credit cards accepted

American's Great
Mistake (Prohibition)
was corrected by the
21st Amendment to the
Constitution, hence the
name of this fine tavern
in the shadow of the
State House. The dark
wood and exposed brick
décor emulates a colo-
nial tavern, right down
to the copper fireplace

(with electric 'fire').
Hoist a few with state
lawmakers as they take
a break from the heavy
lifting of legislation.

Bull & Finch ⑯

84 Beacon St

Ⓣ Subway to Arlington St

Open: daily 1130–2330

All credit cards accepted

Television transformed
this one-time neigh-
bourhood tavern into a
Cheers!-themed amuse-
ment. Bar grub (named
after *Cheers!* characters)
includes the usual

nachos and buffalo
wings as well as clam
chowder. The first line
from the bartender is
usually, 'So where are
you folks from?'

Buzzy's Fabulous Roast Beef ⑰

327 Cambridge St

Ⓣ Subway to Charles/MGH

Open: 24 hours a day

All the night owls come
to roost at Buzzy's, a
garish icon beneath the
Charles/MGH subway
station that serves a
limited menu. Although
they list chicken on a
bun and breakfast egg
sandwiches, the quintes-
sence of Buzzy's is the
roast beef, with or
without grilled onions.

Café Vanille ⑱

70 Charles St

Ⓣ Subway to Charles/MGH

Open: Mon–Fri 0545–1900,
Sat–Sun 0700–1900

Vanille's great strength
is Parisian-style pastries,
sinfully rich with
butter-cream and
ganache (chocolate
cream). They also make
a small selection of
sandwiches on crusty
fresh bread and each
day brings a different
choice of soups and
quiches.

▲ Bull & Finch

▲ Panificio

Derne Street Deli 20

16 Derne St

Ⓢ Subway to Park St

Open: Mon–Thu 0700–2000, Fri–Sat 0700–1800, closed Sun

Tucked behind the State House in an otherwise residential area, Derne Street assembles a broad array of sandwiches and burgers for the luncheon crowd. It's a good spot to pick up the makings of an impromptu picnic.

The Hill Tavern 21

228 Cambridge St

Ⓢ Subway to Charles/MGH

Open: lunch Mon–Fri 1130–1730, Sat–Sun 1500–1730; brunch Sun–Tue 1130–1500; dinner Sun–Tue 1730–2230, Wed–Sat 1730–2300

[VISA] 💳 American Express Discover

A favourite place to hang out for Beacon Hill's moderate-income denizens, the Hill is known for its wood-grilled pizzas. Sandwiches are served until the small hours.

Panificio 22

144 Charles St

Ⓢ Subway to Charles/MGH

Open: Mon–Fri 0700–2200, Sat–Sun 0800–1800

[VISA] 💳

Light meals throughout the day are structured around this bakery's rustic Italian breads. Sandwiches are huge – lots of meat with heaps of salad vegetables. Soups are surprisingly less hearty. Weekend brunches include frittatas, French toast and other eggy dishes.

Paramount Deli Restaurant 23

44 Charles St

Ⓢ Subway to Charles/MGH

Open: breakfast and lunch Mon–Sat 0700–1630, Sun 0800–1630; dinner daily 1730–2200

[VISA] 💳 American Express

A cafeteria-style diner by day, the Paramount has been a comfort-food destination since 1937. Table service takes over at night, with stir fries and demi-bistro dishes (eg, chicken with boursin, topped by a lemon and white wine sauce) still some of the cheapest on the Hill. Good breakfast, too.

Ruby's Café 24

280 Cambridge St

Ⓢ Subway to Charles/MGH

Open: Sun–Wed 0700–2000, Thu–Sat 24 hours a day

All credit cards accepted

It's hard to screw up breakfast, and Ruby's actually makes it a pleasure all day long. Eggs are available in countless permutations with side orders of good pancakes and respectable corned beef hash. Other grill food is also available.

The Sevens 25

77 Charles St

Ⓢ Subway to Charles/MGH

Open: Mon–Sat 1130–0100, Sun 1200–0100

[VISA] 💳 American Express

The Sevens is Beacon Hill's real neighbourhood pub – a well-worn and dark bar with wooden booths and a steady barrage of television. Throw some darts, lift a pint and sup on deli sandwiches.

BEACON HILL
Shops, markets and picnic sites

Shops

De Luca's Market ㉗

11 Charles St

🚇 Subway to Charles/MGH

Open: Mon–Sat 0700–2200,
Sun 0700–2100

💳 American Express

From the street De Luca's looks for all the world like a cute little produce shop with shiny fruits and vegetables in boxes by the windows. Go inside and there's almost any foodstuff that a traveller could desire. True, the extra polish on the apples and the convenience add a bit to the price, but the goods are top quality.

Savenor's ㉖

160 Charles St

🚇 Subway to Charles/MGH

Open: Mon–Fri 0900–2030,
Sat 0900–2000, Sun 0900–1900

💳 American Express

Julia Child, the woman who taught Americans about good food, buys her meat at Savenor's. If you are on a self-catering holiday, you should too. If you are not interested in cooking, then just stop to try some of the spectacular cheeses.

Picnic sites

Boston Common ㉘

Bounded by Park, Tremont, Beacon and Charles Sts

🚇 Subway to Park St

Cows used to graze the Common – now it's people. Enjoy a picnic on the gentle slope above the Frog Pond.

Boston Public Garden ㉙

Bounded by Charles, Beacon, Arlington and Boylston Sts

🚇 Subway to Arlington

The banks of the Garden's lagoon are straight out of Seurat's idylls on the Seine, right down to weeping willows and bobbing ducks.

Bulfinch Circle at the State House ㉚

East side of State House

🚇 Subway to Park St

This miniature park with circular benches used to be the highest point in Boston. Bonfires here warned of attacks, and gave the neighbourhood its name of 'Beacon Hill'. Charles Bulfinch's eagle statue shows the original height of the land. The park is usually sunny and free from the winds that tend to scour other Boston vantage points.

Charles River Esplanade ㉛

Across Arthur Fiedler Footbridge at Arlington and Beacon Sts

🚇 Subway to Charles/MGH

Great cities often grow up on beautiful rivers. Boston's river is the Charles, and the Esplanade was designed with picnics in mind. Pack a lunch (no alcohol allowed) and a blanket for the ground and take in the free entertainment at the Hatch Shell performance stage in the summer.

▲ De Luca's Market

Boston's chain gang

Better the devil you know!

Travellers have good reason for patronising restaurant chains. As a rule, chains specialise in one type of meal and do it very well, providing familiarity and consistency from location to location. The Boston area has been the birthplace of several chain restaurants that offer good prices on their food (all ❺), more character than the usual US fast food chains, and a range of convenient locations around the city. In keeping with their casual nature, none take advance bookings and all will pack up anything on the menu for a takeaway.

Au Bon Pain

Au Bon Pain features freshly made croissants, a few soups and breads. Some locations have become leisurely rest stops akin to Parisian street cafés.
Downtown and Financial District:
• 426 Washington St; ✆ 617-338-0824
• 75 Federal St; ✆ 617-338-5668
• 176 Federal St; ✆ 617-345-9694
• 1 International Pl; ✆ 617-439-0116
• 53 State St; ✆ 617-723-8483
Chinatown and Theatre District:
• 26 Park Plaza; ✆ 617-338-8948
Back Bay and Fenway:
• Prudential Center, 800 Boylston St; ✆ 617-421-9593
• 241 Massachusetts Ave; ✆ 617-267-3524
• 360 Newbury St; ✆ 617-424-7940
Harvard Square:
• 1360 Massachusetts Ave, Cambridge; ✆ 617-661-8738

Bertucci's Brick Oven Pizzeria

With salads and soups, as well as pizzas and baked pastas cooked in a hot brick oven, Bertucci's feels more like a casual Italian restaurant than a mere pizzeria.
Quincy Market and Waterfront:
• Faneuil Hall; ✆ 617-227-7889
Back Bay and Fenway:

▲ Au Bon Pain in Harvard Square

- 43 Stanhope St; ∅ 617-247-6161

Cambridge:
- 21 Brattle St, Harvard Sq; ∅ 617-864-4748
- 799 Main St, Kendall Sq; ∅ 617-661-8356

Boston Market

Roasted chicken and turkey dinners are the main items at Boston Market. Most locations are in the suburbs, except the in-town spot near the Christian Science Church.

Back Bay and Fenway:
- 245 Massachusetts Ave; ∅ 617-236-4447

Jae's

The menu at these casual Asian fusion restaurants ranges from sushi to red and yellow curries, from grilled coconut shrimp and beef *teriyaki* to Korean *kim chee* (fiery fermented cabbage). Many regulars swear by the motto: 'Eat at Jae's and live forever'.

Chinatown and Theatre District:
- 212 Stuart St; ∅ 617-451-7788

South End:
- 520 Columbus Ave; ∅ 617-421-9405

Inman Square:
- 1281 Cambridge St, Cambridge; ∅ 617-497-8380

Pho Pasteur

The beef-noodle soups that will nearly feed two people are among the best-selling dishes at Pho Pasteur, but these restaurants are not just typical Vietnamese soup houses. Their full menu stretches over six pages of Vietnamese dishes – uniformly light, healthy, well seasoned and inexpensive.

Chinatown and Theatre District:
- 682 Washington St; ∅ 617-482-7467

Back Bay and Fenway:
- 119 Newbury St; ∅ 617-262-8200

Harvard Square:
- 36 Dunster St, Cambridge; ∅ 617-864-4100

As a rule, chains specialise in one type of meal and do it very well, providing familiarity and consistency from location to location.

Rebecca's Café

Now owned by Bewley's, the company originating in Dublin, Rebecca's Cafés have a strong local following, specialising in high-quality sandwiches, over-sized cookies, and good pastries. Many locations are in Financial District office buildings and the Café's staff are particularly adept at providing swift service to workers on short lunch breaks. The Harrison Ave location is in a building full of architects, artists and an art gallery.

Downtown and Financial District:
- 18 Tremont St; ∅ 617-227-0020
- 75 Federal St; ∅ 617-482-0066
- 56 High St; ∅ 617-951-2422
- 125 High St; ∅ 617-261-9988
- 75 State St; ∅ 617-261-0022

Back Bay and Fenway:
- 500 Boylston St; ∅ 617-536-5900
- 112 Newbury St; ∅ 617-267-1122
- Prudential Center, 800 Boylston St; ∅ 617-266-3355

South End:
- 560 Harrison Ave; ∅ 617-482-1414.

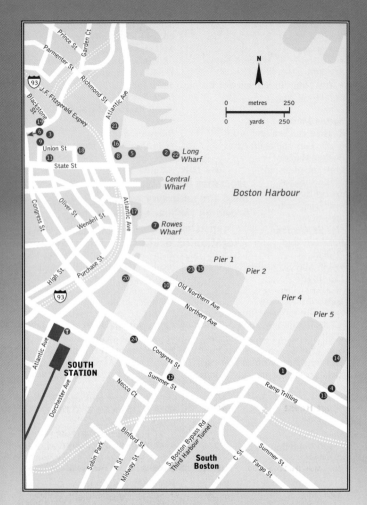

Faneuil Hall Market and Waterfront

More than half the establishments in Faneuil Hall Marketplace sell food of some sort, providing unparalleled choice for casual eating. The waterfront is lined with a lively collection of restaurants, ranging from ultra-casual fish shacks to white-tablecloth fine dining. Logically enough, the waterfront is the smartest place to go for fresh seafood.

FANEUIL HALL MARKET AND WATERFRONT
Restaurants

Aura

Seaport Hotel, 1 Seaport La
⌀ 617-385-4300
Ⓢ Subway to South
Station, shuttle to World
Trade Center

Open: daily 0630–1400,
1730–2200

Reservations recommended

All credit cards accepted

New American

❸❸❸

Subtle and pricey, Aura
is a dining destination
in an area otherwise
known for cheap eats.
Trophy foods dominate
the menu – from
Nantucket bay scallops
to foie gras, local
oysters and rack of
lamb. Great, spicy
desserts add oomph to
the meal.

Chart House Restaurant ❷

60 Long Wharf
⌀ 617-227-1576
Ⓢ Subway to Aquarium

Open: Mon–Thu 1700–2130,
Fri 1700–2300, Sat 1630–
2300, Sun 1630–2130

Reservations recommended

All credit cards accepted

Seafood-American

❸❸❸

The fare at the Chart
House is as conservative
as one might expect
from the 17th-century

red-brick building, the
oldest on Boston's
waterfront. It's the
proper spot for roast
beef, Dover sole or surf-
and-turf (lobster and
steak).

Durgin Park ❸

5 Faneuil Hall Marketplace
⌀ 617-227-2038
Ⓢ Subway to Government
Center or Haymarket

▲ Faneuil Hall Marketplace

Open: Mon–Thu 1130–2200,
Fri–Sat 1130–2230, Sun
1130–2100

Reservations not allowed

All credit cards accepted

American

❸❸

Established in 1826 to
feed produce and meat
market workers, Durgin
Park lives up to its
reputation for generous
portions of American

fare. The upper-level dining room, with its family-style seating, red-and-white checked tablecloths and bentwood chairs, is the best bet for baked beans, cornbread and prime rib that hangs over the edge of the plate.

Jimmy's Harborside ❹

242 Northern Ave
∅ 617-423-1000
⊛ Subway to South Station, shuttle to World Trade Center
Open: Mon–Thu 1200–2130, Fri–Sat 1200–2200, Sun 1600–2100
Reservations recommended

▲ Durgin Park

All credit cards accepted
Seafood
❸❺

Try to get one of the tables at the rear, next to the windows, for a great view of Boston harbour. If you stick to the simplest possible preparations of fresh local fish, you will have as good a time as the entertainment celebrities who left behind signed black-and-white glossy photos which now adorn the walls. Jimmy's dress code is casual.

Kingfish Hall ❸

South Market, Faneuil Hall Marketplace

∅ 617-523-8862
⊛ Subway to Government Center or Haymarket
Open: daily 1100–2200
Reservations not allowed
All credit cards accepted
Seafood
❸❺

With more than 200 seats on two levels and more tables outdoors, Kingfish Hall is the spot to munch your way through a pot of steamed clams or a bowl of seviche at communal tables while a jazz band plays in the corner. Owner Todd English puts an imaginative spin on seafood standards with plates such as wood-grilled lobster tails wrapped in bacon.

Legal Sea Foods ❺

255 State St
∅ 617-227-3115
⊛ Subway to Aquarium
Open: Mon–Fri 1100–2200, Sat 1200–2230, Sun 1200–2100
Reservations not allowed
All credit cards accepted
Seafood
❸❺

At the flagship of the local chain that set Boston's modern standard for fish quality, it is worth waiting to sample Legal's imaginative, eclectic fish dishes. You leave your name at the door and come back when your pocket pager buzzes. Those diners who don't mind sitting with smokers get seated sooner in the bar.

Naked Fish ⑥

16–18 North St

∅ 617-742-3333

⊕ Subway to Government Center or Haymarket

Open: Mon–Sat 1100–2200, Sun 1200–2200

Reservations recommended

▒▒ ⬭ American Express

Seafood

⑤⑤

The name is a cue to eschew the sauces and stick with good (if often farmed) fish brushed with olive oil and lemon before being grilled over an open wood fire. Follow a similar strategy at lunch for a grilled fish steak sandwich.

Rowes Wharf Restaurant ⑦

Boston Harbor Hotel, 70 Rowes Wharf

∅ 617-439-3995

⊕ Subway to Aquarium or South Station

Open: daily 0700–2200

Reservations essential

All credit cards accepted

New American-Seafood

⑤⑤⑤

The high price tends to attract poseurs who like to be seen spending money, but the chef's originality and his obsessive devotion to high-grade ingredients allow serious diners (especially if seated at a harbour-front window table) to ignore the show-offs. Rowes Wharf is among the most accommodating restaurants for diners with

255 State Street · Boston Massachusetts 02109

special requests. The signature lobster sausage is a revelation.

Sel de la Terre ⑧

255 State St

∅ 617-720-1300

⊕ Subway to Aquarium

Open: breakfast Mon–Fri 0630–1030; lunch Mon–Fri 1130–1400; brunch Sat–Sun 0700–1200; dinner daily 1800–2200

Reservations recommended

▒▒ ⬭ American Express

French

⑤⑤⑤

Mopping the broth of your *bouillabaisse* with a sourdough crust is just one of the pleasures of dining on rustic Provençal cuisine at Sel de la Terre. The elegant dining room offers steadily changing à la carte menus, yet you

can get casual breakfast (and picnic bits) at the storefront *boulangerie* and lunch in the bar.

Union Oyster House ⑨

41 Union St

∅ 617-227-2750

⊕ Subway to Government Center or Haymarket

Open: Sun–Thu 1100–2130 Fri–Sat 1100–2200

Reservations recommended

All credit cards accepted

Seafood

⑤⑤

The raw bar is stupendous at this venerable Boston institution. For a touch of history, slip into booth 18 upstairs, where young John F Kennedy used to spend Sunday afternoons reading the newspaper.

FANEUIL HALL MARKET AND WATERFRONT
Bars, cafés and pubs

▲ Bucket of crab claws at Barking Crab

Barking Crab ⑩

88 Sleeper St

🚇 Subway to South Station

Open: Mon–Wed, Sun 1130–2100, Thu–Sat 1130–2200

All credit cards accepted

Open all year, Barking Crab comes into its own with outdoor summer dining at picnic tables, each equipped with a rock to smash crab and lobster shells. Almost every fish in the New England sea is served here, along with some exotics (Alaskan king crab). Steamed clams, the daily special, and a pitcher of beer make an unforgettable meal at this fish shack facing the Financial District skyscrapers.

Black Rose ⑪

160 State St

🚇 Subway to Government Center or Haymarket

Open: Mon–Sat 1130–0200, Sun 1200–0200

All credit cards accepted

Irish-American food hasn't kept up with the advances of real Irish cuisine but the Black Rose is a fine spot to sip a pint of Guinness, enjoy some conversation and catch some Gaelic tunes.

Café Three Hundred 🔞

300 Summer St

🚇 Subway to South Station

Open: Mon–Fri 0830–1530, Sun 0900–1400, closed Sat

💳 🔲 American Express

In an artist-owned studio building, Café Three Hundred nourishes the body the way art nourishes the spirit. Make the midday meal a big one with such dishes as mussel stew with red potatoes, cream and saffron or a roast pork sandwich with eggplant and vinegar peppers.

Il Panino at Faneuil Hall 🟦

120 Faneuil Hall Marketplace

🚇 Subway to Government Center or Haymarket

Open: Mon–Thu, Sun 1100–2200, Fri–Sat 1100–2300

All credit cards accepted

Mix and match pastas, sauces and meats (chicken or veal) for quick and casual dining with the ambience of an up-market bar. Simple pizzas are also good.

Jimbo's 🔞

245 Northern Ave

🚇 Subway to South Station, shuttle to World Trade Center

Open: Mon–Thu 1130–2100, Fri–Sat 1130–2200, Sun 1200–2000

All credit cards accepted

The T-shirt and shorts alternative to **Jimmy's Harborside** (see page 20), Jimbo's strikes a happy medium between a fish shack and white-linen dining. The fish is fresh and cooked exactly right and no one cares if you put your elbows on the table.

No-Name Restaurant 🔞

15 Fish Pier

🚇 Subway to South Station, shuttle to World Trade Center

Open: Mon–Sat 1100–2200, Sun 1130–2100

No credit cards accepted

As bare bones as they come, No Name serves whatever comes in at Fish Pier that day. The clam chowder is usually fantastic. Prices tend to rise slightly at around 1600.

Quincy Market Food Court 🟦

Faneuil Hall Marketplace

🚇 Subway to Government Center or Haymarket

Open: Mon–Sat 0630–2100, Sun 1000–1800

Variety of credit cards

From local fish chowder to pseudo-Mexican fare, almost every form of fast food known to humankind is on offer here. Order what you want and eat at tables beneath the elegant rotunda.

Salty Dog Seafood Bar & Grille 🟦

Faneuil Hall Marketplace

🚇 Subway to Government Center or Haymarket

Open: Mon–Thu 1100–2300, Fri–Sat 1100–2400, Sun 0900–1900

💳 💳 American Express

Although they promote the shore dinners and raw bar (which are indoors), Salty Dog is a great spot to sit outdoors to watch passers-by while enjoying a bluefish sandwich and a bottle of beer.

Sebastian's Café 🔞

US Courthouse, 1 Courthouse Way

🚇 Subway to South Station

Open: Mon–Fri 0700–1530, closed Sat–Sun

💳 💳 American Express

It might seem a hassle to go through a metal detector to reach the courthouse's cafeteria, but the jaw-dropping view of Boston harbour makes it worthwhile, and the sandwiches and soups are excellent.

Tia's at Long Wharf 🔞

200 Atlantic Ave

🚇 Subway to Aquarium

Open: Apr–May Sat–Sun and mid-June–mid-Oct daily 1130–0200

All credit cards accepted

Mid-summer nirvana consists of an unlimited supply of steamed clams and beer and a water-view table on Tia's patio. It can sometimes get a little rowdy during the weekends.

FANEUIL HALL MARKET AND WATERFRONT
Shops, markets and picnic sites

Shops

James Hook & Co

15 Northern Ave

◉ Subway to South Station

Open: Mon–Thu 0600–1700, Fri 0600–1800, Sat 0800–1600, Sun 0800–1300

With the big lobster sign on the weathered side of this Fort Point Channel warehouse, it's not hard to guess Hook's speciality. Moreover, they're well equipped to ship fresh, live New England lobster anywhere in the USA. For more immediate consumption, you could also choose crabs, clams, squid and whatever fish the fleet has just brought in. Prepared lobster bisque and clam chowder are also available.

Kilvert & Forbes ❸

Quincy Market, Faneuil Hall Marketplace

◉ Subway to Government Center or Haymarket

Open: Mon–Sat 0800–2100, Sun 0800–1800

All credit cards accepted

In addition to sinful sweets to eat on the spot, this stall sells New England gift food items that range from Boston Harbour Tea to cans of clam chowder, baked beans, Indian pudding and lobster bisque. They also have maple syrup, beach plum jelly and saltwater taffy.

Rudi's ❶

30 Rowes Wharf

◉ Subway to Aquarium or South Station

Open: Mon–Fri 0730–2000, Sat–Sun 0800–1700

 American Express

Up-market takeaway dinners are Rudi's speciality, though more customers stop by for gourmet deli sandwiches and fancy desserts. The breakfast foods – quiche, pastries and croissants – are tasty too.

Le Saucier ❸

Quincy Market, Faneuil Hall Marketplace

◉ Subway to Government Center or Haymarket

Open: Mon–Sat 1000–2100, Sun 1200–1800

All credit cards accepted

Dedicated to sauces from all over the world, Le Saucier carries an extensive range of the hot pepper and barbecue sauces developed by Boston-area chefs.

Wine Cave ❶

33 Union St

◉ Subway to Government Center or Haymarket

Open: Mon–Thu 0900–2000, Fri–Sat 0900–2300, closed Sun

All credit cards accepted

While there are other wine shops with more elegant (and pricier) stock, the Wine Cave excels in its selection of moderately priced bottles from around the world.

Markets

Haymarket ❶

Blackstone block, rear

◉ Subway to Haymarket

Open: Fri–Sat 0700–1600

Vestigial survivor of the old street markets, Haymarket is a loud, crowded and colourful spot to buy fresh fruits and vegetables for bargain prices. Vendors, not shoppers, usually make the selections, so each tray of berries, for example, might have a few bruised boxes.

Christopher Columbus Park

Between Commercial and Long wharves

Ⓢ Subway to Aquarium

With its decorative pergola and long, low steps, this largely paved park by the waterfront has an Olde Worlde air, and a sense of peace and quiet compared to nearby Faneuil Hall Marketplace. It's a favourite spot for catching midday rays.

Georges Island

Boston harbour

Ⓢ Subway to Aquarium, Harbor Islands Ferry at Long Wharf

Open: May–late-June and early-Sep–mid-Oct Sat–Sun 0900–1800, late-June–early-Sep daily 0900–1800

The largest island in Boston Harbor Islands National Park, Georges has broad greens sweeping down from the fort to the shore – perfect for spreading out a picnic and watching intrepid sailors let their spinnakers loose. The ferry ride (about half an hour each way) is a pleasure, and the view of the city coming back is unsurpassed.

Harborpark

Northern Ave at Fort Point Channel

Ⓢ Subway to South Station

The US government took over one of the prettiest pieces of the waterfront to build a courthouse, but dampened public outrage by landscaping the shore into a fantastic park with great views of the harbour and downtown.

Museum Wharf

Congress St at Fort Point Channel

Ⓢ Subway to South Station

Open: daily 1000–1700

Families visiting the Children's Museum in the old wool warehouses at Fort Point Channel will find pleasant outdoor eating areas near the front entrance. A few fast-food vendors, including the Hood Milk Bottle, share the area, but visitors are welcome to bring their own repasts.

▲ Faneuil Hall Marketplace

Go Fish

Fantastic fish fare

Whimsy has nothing to do with the gilded wooden codfish that hangs prominently in the Massachusetts State House. The icon is known as the 'sacred cod', for Boston's first fortunes were made in the cod trade and the oldest moneyed families were known as the 'codfish aristocracy'. The rich fishing banks only a few miles from the mouth of Boston harbour are recovering strongly from overfishing, and the inshore fisheries all along the New England coast yield hefty catches of fish and shellfish alike.

Boston Fish Pier, built between 1912 and 1915, remains the oldest active fish pier in the USA, and the size of the catch and the resulting prices at the morning fish auction often dictate that night's 'specials' menu at up to a third of the

city's restaurants. Many seafood restaurants naturally cluster near Fish Pier. Two restaurants exemplify the extremes of serving style. Actually on the pier is the no-nonsense **No-Name Restaurant** (*see page 23*), where you could easily be dining with fishermen having a bite to eat before they go out to sea again. By contrast, **Anthony's Pier 4** (*140 Northern Ave; ✆ 617-423-6363;* ❸❸❸) combines one of the most striking views of Boston harbour with an old-fashioned, big-production restaurant where plain fish is given the royal treatment. Anthony's is most famous for the celebrities who have eaten there – autographed photos of movie stars and politicians are plastered all over the entrance area.

Several other fish restaurants inhabit the Fish Pier area. Chinese dishes employing local species are the speciality at **Eastern Pier Seafood Restaurant** (*237 Northern Ave; ✆ 617-423-7756;* ❸❸), while Southern Italian plates, especially squid, are the mainstay of **The Daily Catch** (*261 Northern Ave, ✆ 617-338-3093 and 323 Hanover St, ✆ 617-523-8560; American Express and cash only;* ❸). Take note that it can take up to two hours queuing to eat at the Hanover St (North End) location, as the seating is extremely limited in this popular spot.

▲ Live lobster

Virtually every restaurant in Boston features fish prominently. Among those whose menu is almost entirely seafood, the city's acknowledged leader is the hydra-headed **Legal Sea Foods** (*see page 20; 26 Park Pl, ℘ 617-426-4444; Prudential Center, 800 Boylston St, ℘ 617-266-6800; Copley Place, 100 Huntington Ave, ℘ 617-266-7775; 5 Cambridge Center, Kendall Sq, Cambridge, ℘ 617-864-3400; no reservations; ❸❸*), which set the standard for fastidious fish handling and straightforward preparations. The Long Wharf restaurant, right in front of the New England Aquarium, and the new restaurant at Park Plaza in the Theatre District are destination dining spots. Those at the Prudential Center and Copley Place malls are convenient for shoppers who need a break.

Jasper White's **Summer Shack** (*100 Alewife Brook Prkwy, Cambridge; ℘ 617-520-9500; ❸❸*) offers casual seafood, one of Boston's finest raw bars and a daily selection of inspired fish presentations at an oddly inland location adjacent to the Alewife junction, just three stops from Harvard Square. One of the region's leading chefs and a key player in upgrading Boston dining, White is a stickler for quality and freshness. Despite the name, the restaurant is open all year.

Seafood diners who also wish to angle for company should

Boston's first fortunes were made in the cod trade and the oldest moneyed families were known as the 'codfish aristocracy'.

consider the lively bar scenes at **Skipjack's Seafood Emporium** (*500 Boylston St; ℘ 617-536-3500; ❸❸*) and **Atlantic Fish Company** (*761 Boylston St; ℘ 617-267-4000; ❸❸*). Atlantic Fish also offers pavement tables for diners who wish to take part in the Back Bay's street milieu. At the Back Bay edge of South End, the convivial **Grillfish** (*162 Columbus Ave; ℘ 617-357-1620*), with its stylish large bar and open kitchen, keeps fish preparations simple and can boast the hottest singles scene of all the fish houses.

Beach areas north and south of the city are rife with 'clam shacks' – casual seafood restaurants with picnic tables. Only one flourishes in town: **Barking Crab** (*see page 22*) on Fort Point Channel.

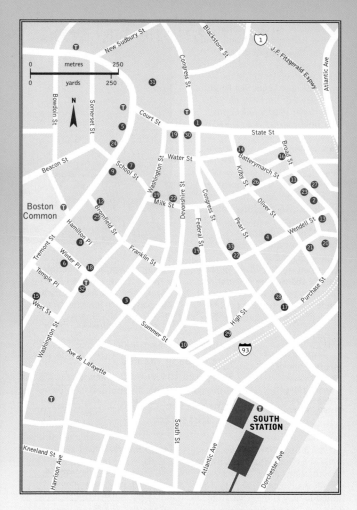

Downtown and Financial District

Because the Downtown and adjacent Financial District are Boston's business centres, they are rich with lunch spots offering good deals on above-average meals on weekdays. The bar scene comes alive immediately after work, then quietens down until a high-rolling clientele begin to fill some of the city's splashiest destination restaurants.

DOWNTOWN AND FINANCIAL DISTRICT
Restaurants

Bay Tower

60 State St (33rd floor)

✆ 617-723-1666

Ⓜ Subway to Government Center

Open: Mon–Fri 1730–2145, Sat 1700–2215, closed Sun

Reservations recommended

All credit cards accepted

French-New American

💲💲💲

Pricey luxuries dominate the menu, such as a lobster and *foie gras* terrine followed by sea bass dressed with osetra caviar. But diners can save a few dollars by ordering from the abridged but still ambitious menu in the upstairs lounge, where the jaw-dropping view of Boston harbour is slightly better and there's live music from Monday to Saturday.

Caliterra ②

Wyndham Hotel, 89 Broad St

✆ 617-556-0006

Ⓜ Subway to South Station

Open: breakfast and lunch 0630–1430; dinner 1700–2230

Reservations recommended

All credit cards accepted

New American-Italian

💲💲💲

The Wyndham Hotel people say the cuisine is Californian, but that's more a matter of the provenance of the wines, produce and even some of the meats. Emphasis in the snazzy, art-deco room is on light and tasty fare such as shrimp in crispy filo pastry and big salads.

Dakota's ③

101 Arch St

✆ 617-737-1777

Ⓜ Subway to Downtown Crossing

Open: Mon–Fri lunch 1130–1500; dinner 1700–2200; closed Sat–Sun

Reservations recommended

All credit cards accepted

New American

💲💲💲

Hidden away on an upper level, Dakota's is a civilised retreat from Downtown Crossing's bustle. The menu mixes up textures and flavours to good effect in dishes such as crunchy grilled shrimp with tropical fruit salsa. 'Twilight' *prix fixe* from 1700 to 1830 offers limited choice but good value.

Julien ④

Hotel Meridien, 250 Franklin St

✆ 617-451-1900

Ⓜ Subway to South Station

Open: lunch Mon–Sat 1200–1400; dinner 1800–2200; closed Sun

Reservations essential

All credit cards accepted

French

💲💲💲

Formal, elegant, and so incredibly French, the Julien makes no concessions to squeamish American tastes, happily serving musky terrines, soup dressed with

maison robert

▲ Lunchtime at Sakura-Bana Japanese Restaurant

truffles, and rabbit fricassee with eggplant and Provençal olives. Superb professional waiters complete the experience ... at a significant price.

Kinsale Irish Pub & Restaurant ❺

2 Center Plaza

∅ 617-742-5577

🚇 Subway to Government Center

Open: Sun–Mon 1100–2230, Tue–Sat 1100–2300

Reservations not allowed

All credit cards accepted

Irish

❸❺

Kinsale's owners brought the pub over brick by brick from Ireland, and perhaps the menu as well, word for word. Casual (and normally packed) by day, the restaurant grows a touch more decorous by evening and for weekend brunch. The four-onion soup is a great winter warmer and the rafters ring with lively Irish music several days a week.

Locke-Ober ❻

3 Winter Pl

∅ 617-542-1340

🚇 Subway to Park St

Open: lunch Mon–Fri 1130–1430; dinner Mon–Sat 1730–2230; closed Sun

Reservations recommended

All credit cards accepted

American-French

❸❸❺

A bastion of old Boston, Locke-Ober didn't allow women in the door until 1970. Old-style French gourmet specials are available, but most of the menu leans toward simple Dover sole or dry-aged sirloin steak. The gleaming woodwork and silver would be blinding if they turned up the lights.

Maison Robert ❼

45 School St

✆ 617-227-8600

🔴 Subway to Park St

Open: lunch Mon Sat 1130–1430; dinner Mon–Sat 1730–2130; closed Sun

Reservations recommended

All credit cards accepted

French

💲💲💲

Classical French haute cuisine meets a radical young master in chef Jacky Robert, although the overdressed dining room (and overdressed patrons) appears to come straight from the late 19th century. For much lower-priced bistro dishes with flair, head downstairs to Ben's Café, which sets up outdoor tables by the statue of Ben Franklin during warm weather.

Marliave Restaurant ❽

31 Bromfield St

✆ 617 423-6340

🔴 Subway to Park St

Open: Mon–Thu 1100–2130, Fri–Sat 1100–2230, closed Sun

Reservations unnecessary

▭ ▭ American Express Discover

Italian

💲💲

Atmospheric and quaint, Marliave serves large portions of lightly seasoned Italian-American fare: heavily breaded veal, good broiled fish, long-cooked vegetables, and pastas with lots of red sauce.

Parker's Restaurant ❾

60 School St

✆ 617-227-8600

🔴 Subway to Park St

Open: breakfast and lunch Mon–Fri 0700–1400, Sat–Sun 0700–1400; dinner daily 1730–2230

Reservations recommended

All credit cards accepted

American

💲💲💲

Boston's literati of the 1870s dined here regularly, and the menu has a timeless New England quality. Baked scrod, Parker House rolls and Boston cream pie were invented in this kitchen and are still on the menu. John F Kennedy's politically astute grandfather made Parker's the de facto Democratic Party headquarters, and state government wheelers and dealers still dine here in time-honoured tradition.

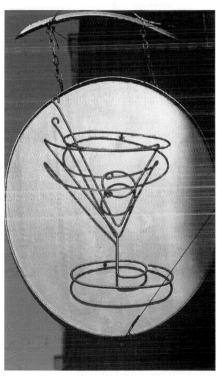

Radius 🔟

8 High St

✆ 617-426-1234

🔘 Subway to South Station

Open: lunch Mon–Fri 1130–1430; dinner Mon–Sat 1730–2200; closed Sun

Reservations essential

All credit cards accepted

New American

❸❸❸

Painted in a Rolls-Royce palette, Radius is dedicated to the expensive exploration of novel culinary trends. Chef and co-owner Michael Schlow manages to make them work with explosive sensuality and attention to minute detail, pairing, for example, slow-roasted sturgeon with Chinese mustard greens. Lone diners can join the convivial crowd at an elevated bar in one corner of the room.

Sakura-Bana Japanese Restaurant ⑪

57 Broad St

✆ 617-542-4311

🔘 Subway to South Station

Open: lunch Mon–Fri 1130–1430; dinner daily 1700–2200

Reservations recommended (for dinner). Reservations not allowed (lunch)

All credit cards accepted

Japanese

❷❺

Sakura-Bana can barely keep up with the lunch crowd, half of whom come to pick up a take-away, the other half to trade stock tips. Sushi's the main attraction at lunch. Cooked dishes dominate the dinner menu.

Silvertone Bar & Grill ⑫

69 Bromfield St

✆ 617-338-7887

🔘 Subway to Park St or Downtown Crossing

Open: Mon–Fri 1130–2230, Sat 1730–2230, closed Sun

All credit cards accepted

American

❷❺

Retro cool ambience – as in 1950s jazz and dense clouds of cigarette smoke – overshadows such updated American classics as meatloaf served with broccoli *rabe* sautéed with lots of garlic.

Trattoria Il Panino ⑬

295 Franklin St

✆ 617-338-1000

🔘 Subway to South Station

Open: Mon–Fri 1130–0200, Sat 1730–0200, closed Sun

Reservations recommended (for restaurant). Reservations not allowed (for bistro)

All credit cards accepted

Italian

❷❺

Diners can opt for pizzas and pastas at the ground level bistro or climb the stairs to a serious Italian restaurant with an innovative menu.

Vault Restaurant ⑭

105 Water St

✆ 617-292-9966

🔘 Subway to Government Center

Open: lunch Mon–Fri 1130–1430; dinner Mon–Sat 1730–2230; closed Sun

Reservations recommended

All credit cards accepted

New American

❸❸❸

Located literally in a bank vault, this sterling example of New American tastes (chicken livers breaded with chopped filberts) also boasts an exquisite and reasonably priced wine list. A limited late night bar menu is available from Thursday to Saturday.

West Street Grille ⑮

15 West St

✆ 617-423-0300

🔘 Subway to Downtown Crossing

Open: lunch Mon–Fri 1130–1530; dinner Mon–Sat 1730–2200; closed Sun

Reservations recommended

💳 💳 American Express

New American

❷❺

Not just another grill to feed the drinkers at the bar, West Street invests culinary care in everything from grilled salmon and yellow fin tuna to beef fillet and pork tenderloin.

DOWNTOWN AND FINANCIAL DISTRICT
Bars, cafés and pubs

Bakey's 16

45 Broad St

🚇 Subway to South Station

Open: Mon–Fri 1130–2000, closed Sat–Sun

American Express

Wooden booths make a nicer than usual setting for soup and sandwiches at lunch or casual pub fare in the evening.

Carl's Deli 17

147 Pearl St

🚇 Subway to South Station

Open: Mon–Fri 0430–1600, Sat 0430–1330, closed Sun

No credit cards accepted

Contemporary diner designers can't touch the authenticity of Carl's, where *cognoscenti* head for dawn breakfasts.

Corner Mall 18

Corner of Washington and Winter Sts

🚇 Subway to Downtown Crossing

Open: Mon–Sat 0700–1830, Sun 1200–1800

Variety of credit cards

This food court emphasises healthier choices than most, including a salad booth and a Greek cart with good *souvlaki*.

Cosí 19

133 Federal St; 53 State St; 14 Milk St

🚇 Subway to South Station; to State; to Downtown Crossing

Open: Mon–Fri 0700–1700, closed Sat–Sun

All credit cards accepted

Super-fresh Italian flat breads, baked continuously on site, are swiftly filled to order with delectable vegetables, meats and cheeses. The Federal St shop has a great outdoor patio.

Country Life Vegetarian 20

200 High St

🚇 Subway to South Station

Open: lunch Sun 1000–1500, Mon–Fri 1130–1500; dinner Sun, Tue–Thu 1700–2000; closed Sat

American Express

▲ Lunch at the International Place Food Court

▲ Rockin' at the Rainbow Rollers Café

Acceptable pizza and *calzones* and big plates of well-sauced pasta are the mainstays at Rico, a handsome hall that teems at midday and grows quiet in the afternoon.

Rainbow Rollers Café 26

7 Liberty Sq

◉ Subway to Government Center

Open: Mon–Fri 1100–1400

No credit cards accepted

Join the brokerage workers streaming out of their offices and grab a grilled chicken breast and salad wrapped in a flour tortilla for the latest lunch craze from California.

Sultan's Kitchen 27

72 Broad St

◉ Subway to South Station

Open: Mon–Fri 1100–1700, Sat 1100–1500, closed Sun

[VISA] [card] American Express

Regulars swear by the lamb *shish* kebab but such dishes as cold eggplant stuffed with onion, tomatoes, parsley and garlic will please vegetarians as well.

Viga 28

133 Pearl St

◉ Subway to South Station

Open: Mon–Fri 1100–1600

No credit cards accepted

Sandwiches and baked pastas are practically a steal at the smartly turned out Viga. The artichoke pizzas are not bad either!

Cafeteria-style service keeps prices rock bottom for vegetarian fare with a Middle-Eastern bent.

International Place Food Court 21

Corner of Oliver St and High St

◉ Subway to South Station

Open: Mon–Fri 0700–1600, closed Sat–Sun

Variety of credit cards

Tables grouped around a sunny atrium with a waterfall make this a genuinely classy spot for a cheap lunch.

Milk Street Café 22

50 Milk St; Post Office Sq Park

◉ Subway to State; to South Station

Open: Mon–Fri 0700–1500, closed Sat–Sun; Mon–Fri 0700–1700, closed Sat–Sun

No credit cards accepted

The original is a dairy kosher sandwich shop (known for egg and tuna salads), while the Post Office Square Park outpost adds summer-time carts selling hot dogs, ice cream and deli meat sandwiches.

Mr Dooley's Boston Tavern 23

77 Broad St

◉ Subway to South Station

Open: daily 1130–0200

All credit cards accepted

This vestige of Boston's Irish lace-curtain brigade has good beer, acceptable pub grub and frequent entertainment.

New York Soup Exchange 24

3 Center Plaza, Government Center

◉ Subway to Government Center

Open: Mon–Fri 0700–1900, Sat 0900–1100, closed Sun

No credit cards accepted

Good soup comes with a freshly baked roll and piece of fruit. Vegetarian, low fat and dairy-free choices are always available. This popular spot has limited seating.

Pizzeria Rico 25

32 Bromfield St

◉ Subway to Park St

Open: Mon–Fri 1000–1800, Sat 1000–1700

All credit cards accepted

DOWNTOWN AND FINANCIAL DISTRICT
Shops, markets and picnic sites

Shops

Au Chocolat 29

35 High St

◉ Subway to South Station

Open: Mon–Fri 0730–1800, closed Sat–Sun

American Express Discover

Despite its French name, Au Chocolat is one of Boston's older-style chocolatiers, fashioning such popular treats as bonbons with mixed fillings and pretzels coated with white, milk or dark chocolate – all available by the pound.

Federal Wine & Spirits 30

29 State St

◉ Subway to State or Government Center

Open: Mon–Fri 0900–1900, Sat 1100–1800, closed Sun

American Express Discover

Boasting one of the broader selections of fine distilled spirits as well as more than 1000 wines, Federal's small store belies its deep cellars, which cater to the downtown law offices and brokerage houses.

Markets

Scollay Square Farmers' Market 31

Government Center, City Hall Plaza

◉ Subway to Government Center

Open: July–Oct, Mon and Wed 1100–1800

No credit cards accepted

Disreputable Scollay Square, torn down in the 1950s, survives in name only at this good market, which attracts fruit, produce and flower growers from up to 100 miles away. Local corn (maize) and tomatoes, often too delicate or too ripe to export, are always in demand. In August arrive early before the tiny, sweet peaches sell out.

Picnic sites

Downtown Crossing 32

Junction of Summer, Winter and Washington Sts

◉ Subway to Downtown Crossing

This pedestrianised square has been the heart of Boston's downtown since 1630. Most folks purchase burritos, drinks, hot dogs and other standard street fare from pushcarts and find a bench to enjoy lunch in the sun.

Post Office Square Park 33

Bounded by Congress, Pearl, Milk, Franklin Sts

◉ Subway to State or Government Center

This beautiful green triangle surrounded by architectural landmark buildings in the heart of the Financial District almost makes up for Downtown's lack of parks. It is easily the best midday picnic site in the middle of the city. Bring your own or purchase sandwiches from the **Milk Street Café** kiosk (*see page 34*).

▲ Picnicking in Post Office Square Park

Business and pleasure

Catering for capitalists

Boston business concerns have traditionally focused on providing investment capital, legal advice, transport, telecommunications, and scientific and technological know-how – precisely the critical elements in the 21st-century economy. Business people from around the globe come to Boston to negotiate and consummate deals.

Many different kinds of restaurants cultivate this business clientele. There are restaurants well suited to discussions (hushed and private), places where company representatives converge to seal a deal (usually more public), and those special restaurants where the principals repair to celebrate a financial coup.

Only a handful of fine Boston restaurants really fit the bill for celebrating a successful IPO (Initial Public Offering of stock) or a billion-dollar merger.

Locales that spark thinking 'outside the box' in order to structure a deal.

The Fed (*see page 10*) is only too happy to oblige the conspicuous consumer. In addition to a gourmet tasting menu priced well above $100 per person, The Fed has a wine cellar filled with rare vintages purchased at auction.

If lawyers and investment capitalists like The Fed, entrepreneurs and inventors favour **L'Espalier** (*see page 51*), the first choice of newly minted millionaires with refined tastes. If The Fed were a Rolls Royce, then L'Espalier would be a Lamborghini.

By those same terms, the **Julien** restaurant (*see page 29*) would be a top-of-the-range Citroën. The Julien occupies the former Federal Reserve Bank building, where the US government once kept cash for distribution to the Boston economy. International deals, especially with Asian companies, are often toasted here.

And if that toast includes a fine cigar, the admittedly less sumptuous but smoke-friendly confines of **Grill 23 & Bar** (*161 Berkeley St; ✆ 617-542-2255;* ❸❸❸) might fit the bill. Their legendary steaks appeal to many economic Darwinists.

Boston is also rich with business restaurants that feature more adventurous food and assertive

décor – locales that spark thinking 'outside the box' in order to structure a deal. **Ambrosia on Huntington** (*116 Huntington Ave; ✆ 617-247-2400; lunch Mon–Fri, dinner daily;* ❸❸❸) is the perfect spot to impress a client or potential partner with your creativity by association, whereas **Café Louis** (*234 Berkeley St; ✆ 617-266-4680; lunch and dinner Mon–Sat, closed Sun;* ❸❸❸) combines chic culinary invention with the aura of Old-Boston prestige in the former Museum of Natural History edifice in Back Bay.

Closer to the Financial District action, Boston's biggest bankers dine at **Radius** (*see page 31*), their appetites whetted from recent take-overs. A business group reservation at **Vault Restaurant** (*see page 32*) is like money in the bank. It's near the Boston firm that invented mutual fund investments.

Those who make and practise the law have their own dining spots. State lawmakers traditionally hang out at **The Last Hurrah** (*Omni Parker House Hotel, 60 School St; ✆ 617-227-8600;* ❸❸), named after a *roman à clef* about Boston politics. But if they want a more serious meal, they head to **No 9 Park** (*see page 11*). So many lawyers drop in after work at **Black Rhino** (*21 Broad St; ✆ 617-263-0101; closed Sun;* ❸❸) that it's been dubbed the 'Ally McBeal bar', after the TV series. To schmooze with the legal beagles, stay downstairs and order from the bar menu.

In the age of geek empowerment, favourite restaurants of the computer

programmers and biotech specialists have acquired significant cachet. Coders – known more for programming expertise than their ability to distinguish foods – fuel up at the **Blue Diner** (*see page 43*), conveniently open around the clock. The more discerning genomics and artificial intelligence experts, by contrast, admire the subtle inventions at **Salts** (*798 Main St, Cambridge; ✆ 617-876-8444; closed Mon;* ❸❸❸).

The three-martini lunch is passé in many business circles, but the formal afternoon tea has taken its place. Two of Boston's finest are found at the **Bristol Lounge** (*Four Seasons Hotel, 200 Boylston St; ✆ 617-338-4400; booking recommended;* ❸) and the **Ritz Carlton Hotel** (*15 Arlington St; ✆ 617-536-5700; booking recommended;* ❸).

Chinatown and Theatre District

Chinatown is one of the best Boston neighbourhoods for inexpensive and late-night dining. The cuisine has followed the demographics of immigration and now embraces much of Asia's Pacific Rim. Look to the adjacent Theatre District for some of Boston's most stylish dining, to the Leather District for chic bistros and forever-open diners.

CHINATOWN AND THEATRE DISTRICT
Restaurants

Aujourd'hui ❶

200 Boylston St

✆ 617-451-1392

Ⓢ Subway to Arlington

Open: breakfast Mon–Fri 0630–1100, Sat 0700–1200, Sun 0700–1100; lunch Sun–Fri 1130–1300; dinner Mon–Sat 1730–2200, Sun 1800–2200

Reservations essential

All credit cards accepted

New American-French

❸❸❸

One of Boston's most elegant formal dining rooms, Aujourd'hui is often fully booked for dinner. Lunch, however, can be a decidedly up-market treat. This is a popular restaurant for celebrating wedding anniversaries and closing major business deals.

Biba ❷

272 Boylston St

✆ 617-426-7878

Ⓢ Subway to Arlington

Open: lunch Sun–Fri 1130–1400; dinner Sun–Thu 1730–2130, Fri–Sat 1730–2230

Reservations essential

All credit cards accepted

New American

❸❸❸

Smart and sassy, Biba marries a bright and rather casual décor with a pricey menu of quirky dishes that appeal to avant-garde diners. Chef-owners Lydia Shire

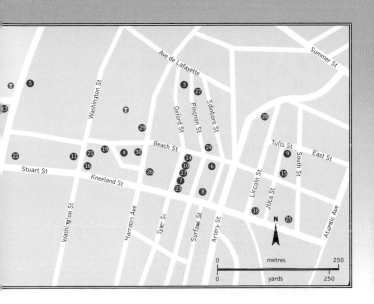

and Susan Regis are regularly celebrated as some of the best in the USA, and Biba is their showcase for imaginative treatments. It is probably the only spot in Boston where offal is always on offer.

Chau Chow City Restaurant ⑤

83 Essex St

☎ 617-338-8158

Ⓢ Subway to Chinatown

Open: Sun–Thu 0830–0300, Fri–Sat 0830–0400

Reservations not allowed

VISA ⊕ American Express

Chinese

Ⓢ

The lower two floors specialise in modern Hong Kong seafood

▲ *Dim sum* in Chinatown

272 Boylston Street

Boston

Massachusetts 02116

617 • 426 • 7878

dishes (such as scallops with green beans and macadamia nuts), while the top level is among Boston's best *dim sum* palaces. The shrimp dumpling is the *dim sum* benchmark, and this one is a perfect tender wrapper around a sweet and crunchy shrimp.

East Ocean City 4

27 Beach St

✆ 617-542-2504

🚇 Subway to Chinatown

Open: Mon–Thu, Sun 1100–0300, Fri–Sat 1100–0400

Reservations not allowed

Chinese-Seafood

Diners needn't worry about freshness at East Ocean City, as the main course is swimming in tanks just inside the front door. Cantonese seafood is the emphasis here, but the vast menu also includes many pork, chicken and beef dishes and vegetarian choices.

Galleria Italiana 5

177 Tremont St

✆ 617-423-2092

🚇 Subway to Boylston

Open: breakfast and lunch 0700–1500; dinner Tue–Sat 1730–2200

Reservations essential

All credit cards accepted

Italian

💲💲

With good muffins and great coffee in the morning and fresh pastas served cafeteria-style at midday, Galleria Italiana dresses up for the evening with a sophisticated Abruzzi menu and an excellent wine list, drawn from the Adige valley and the Piedmont.

Ginza Japanese Restaurant 6

16 Hudson St

✆ 617-338-2261

🚇 Subway to Chinatown

Open: lunch Mon–Fri 1130–1430, Sat–Sun 1130–1600; dinner Sun–Mon 1700–0200, Tue–Sat 1700–0400

Reservations not allowed

All credit cards accepted

Japanese

💲💲

Ginza evokes a little bit of Tokyo far from home, right down to waitresses in kimonos. Sushi are the main attraction, especially among the late-night crowd, and Ginza's chefs are locally famous for their *maki* rolls. Japanese hot pots are also prepared at the table.

New Peking Cuisine Restaurant 7

10 Tyler St

✆ 617-542-5857

🚇 Subway to Chinatown

Open: Sun–Thu 1130–2230, Fri–Sat 1130–2430

Reservations not allowed

All credit cards accepted

Chinese

$$

The name is misleading, as it suggests the Mandarin court cuisine of China's capital. But the fare at New Peking is primarily Szechuan – redolent of hot peppers, strong spices and meat instead of fish. This stylish restaurant attracts an eclectic international crowd.

New Shanghai Restaurant

21 Hudson St

✆ 617-338-6688

⊛ Subway to Chinatown

Open: Sun–Thu 1130–2200, Fri–Sat 1130–2300

Reservations recommended

All credit cards accepted

Chinese

$$

With white-linen table-cloths, New Shanghai aims for modern elegance. Hong Kong-trained C K Sau's lusty modern cooking (such as baby eels in orange sauce) blends invention with tradition. Some of Boston's top non-Chinese chefs dine here for inspiration.

Oskar's ⑨

107 South St

✆ 617-542-6756

⊛ Subway to South Station

Open: lunch Mon–Fri 1130–1400; dinner Tue–Wed 1730–2200, Thu–Fri 1730–2300, Sat 1900–2300; closed Sun

Reservations recommended

All credit cards accepted

New American

$$

Late-1990s decadence and Trash Art décor suit the Leather District's dot-com types well. Order killer martinis and good noshes (grilled pizzas, baked *chèvre*, etc) at the bar, and luscious bistro-trattoria fare (such as duck risotto) at the tables.

Peach Farm Restaurant ⑩

4 Tyler St

✆ 617-482-1116

⊛ Subway to Chinatown

Open: daily 1100–0200

Reservations recommended

All credit cards accepted

Chinese-Seafood

$

When suburban Chinese families are willing to brave Chinatown parking to go out to eat, the restaurant has to be special. For fans of Cantonese delicacies (eg, sesame-tossed jelly-fish with sweet *daikon* pickles), Peach Farm is a must.

Penang ⑪

685 Washington St

✆ 617 451-6373

⊛ Subway to Chinatown

Open: Sun–Thu 1030–2330, Fri–Sat 1130–2400

▲ Rice plates come round at Chau Chow City

2 Tyler St

⌀ 617-423-3889

Ⓜ Subway to Chinatown

Open: daily 1100–0200

Reservations recommended

American Express

Korean-Japanese

❷❸

Like most Korean restaurants in Boston, Suishaya concentrates as much on sushi as the hearty soups and stews of Korea. Gorge on sushi from Sunday to Thursday at an all-you-can-eat fixed price. There's a great deal on bento box specials at noon and midnight.

Les Zygomates Wine Bar & Bistro ⓯

129 South St

⌀ 617-542-5108

Ⓜ Subway to South Station

Open: lunch Mon–Fri 1130–1400; dinner Mon–Sat 1800–2230; café menu 2230–2430; closed Sun

Reservations recommended

All credit cards accepted

French

❷❸

Named after the facial muscles essential for smiling, Les Zyg usually uncorks more than 40 bottles of good wine at a time for drinks by the glass. The food is straightforward French bistro cuisine, and one side of the restaurant has live jazz six nights a week. Piaf's here, if only in spirit.

Reservations not allowed

Malay-Indian-Thai

❸

Malay is the mother cuisine of Southeast Asian cooking, and Penang packs in crowds for relatively inexpensive noodle plates, steamed fish dishes and such inventions as chicken in a hot, sweet-and-sour mango sauce.

Pignoli ⓬

91 Park Plaza

⌀ 617-338-7500

Ⓜ Subway to Arlington

Open: lunch Mon–Sat 1130–1430; dinner Sun–Thu 1730–2200, Fri–Sat 1730–2300

Reservations recommended

All credit cards accepted

New American-Italian

❸❸❸

Pignoli's contemporary, inventive Italian menu (with a spectacular *antipasti* selection) is especially inviting in warm weather when you can sit outside at café tables. The interior décor remains pure late-1980s Milanese, with a very international bar scene.

Pravda 116 ⓭

116 Boylston St

⌀ 617-482-7799

Ⓜ Subway to Boylston

Open: Tue–Sat 1700–2200, closed Sun–Mon

Reservations recommended

All credit cards accepted

New American

❷❸

Don't let the dance club and the I'm-too-sexy bar distract you from some of the Theatre District's best, most imaginative cooking at fair prices. Any wood-grilled main course is a solid bet – generally it is hearty fare with finesse.

CHINATOWN AND THEATRE DISTRICT
Bars, cafés and pubs

Banh Mi 16

696 Washington St

🚇 Subway to Chinatown

Open: daily 0800–1700

No credit cards accepted

Although there's some seating at Banh Mi, the primary business is in takeaways. The tiny eatery offers meatballs, sticky rice in banana leaves, dumplings and the like, but most customers opt for the delicious pork or vegetarian Vietnamese sandwiches, spurning McDonald's next door.

Best Café 17

11 Tyler St

🚇 Subway to Chinatown

Open: daily 0800–0200

VISA 🔴 American Express
Discover

The garish décor is as authentically Hong Kong as the vast menu at Best Café, where the big portions of Chinese food, low prices and late hours make it a magnet for students. There are good deals to be had on multi-course dinners for two, four, six or eight diners.

Blue Diner 18

150 Kneeland St

🚇 Subway to South Station

Open: 24 hours a day

VISA 🔴 American Express

Blue may be a faux diner, but it seats more people than the nearby South Street Diner. After a little local clubbing, it's the perfect place to sober up on a midnight meatloaf or passable barbecue before figuring out how to get home.

Buddha's Delight Vegetarian Restaurant 19

5 Beach St

🚇 Subway to Chinatown

Open: Sun–Thu 1100–2130, Fri–Sat 1100–2230

VISA 🔴

Buddha's Delight is one place where vegetarians can take their carnivore friends, since the kitchen delights in creating Chinese and Vietnamese meat analogues with soy and wheat proteins. The second-storey dining room has a good vantage on the busy street scene.

Finale 20

15 Columbus Ave

🚇 Subway to Arlington

Open: Mon 1130–2200, Tue–Fri 1130–2400, Sat 1800–2400, Sun 1600–2300

All credit cards accepted

Finale's forte is pre- and post-theatre desserts and drinks, but it can be a very good spot to pick up a sandwich before picnicking in the public garden or to enjoy a dinner before a play.

Hù Tiêu Nam-Vang 21

7 Beach St

🚇 Subway to Chinatown

Open: Sun–Thu 0830–2200, Fri–Sat 0800–2230

No credit cards accepted

▲ Vietnamese restaurants are proliferating

▲ Jacob Wirth attracts crowds every day

The Vietnamese rice and noodle plates are astonishingly good deals, though it can be hard to get a seat for lunch when every office or construction worker in Chinatown is waiting to order. Excellent beef and tendon soup (with basil and bean sprouts on the side) comes in bowls big enough to feed two.

Jacob Wirth Company ㉒

31–7 Stuart St

🚇 Subway to Boylston

Open: Sun–Mon 1130–2000, Tue–Thu and Sat 1130–2200, Fri 1130–2400

All credit cards accepted

In a city overloaded with Mediterranean dining, Jacob Wirth's stands out as the only place where *Bratwurst* with sauerkraut and homemade potato salad is standard fare. The *Sauerbraten* may not be up to Munich standards, but the price is right and the atmosphere authentic. After all, it's been around since 1868.

King Fung Garden ㉓

74 Kneeland St

🚇 Subway to Chinatown

Open: daily 1100–2200

No credit cards accepted

Bring your own alcoholic beverages

The red vinyl seats and claustrophobic room aren't the prettiest, but aficionados of northern Chinese cuisines (including many non-Chinese Boston chefs) keep King Fung busy. Although more expensive than the rest of the menu, Mongolian fire pots are the big draw.

Rainbow Restaurant ㉔

60 Beach St

🚇 Subway to Chinatown

Open: daily 0900–2300

No credit cards accepted

The Rainbow is tops in Chinatown for simple roast duck but it also roasts chicken and slabs of pork spare ribs. The Chinese meat and rice plates are a steal, but most customers buy whole poultry or rib slabs for takeaways. Seating is very limited.

South Street Diner ㉕

178 Kneeland St

🚇 Subway to South Station

Open: 24 hours a day

No credit cards accepted

It's hard to squeeze into this tiny diner, but the breakfast menu is good around the clock and the hamburgers and cheeseburgers have an old-fashioned authenticity you won't find at the chains.

CHINATOWN AND THEATRE DISTRICT
Shops, markets and picnic sites

Shops

Chang Kwong Seafood Market

73–9 Essex St

🚇 Subway to Chinatown

Open: daily 0830–1930

Granted, most self catering units lack the kitchen facilities to do justice to the live fish at Chang Kwong, but the market also carries an extensive range of fresh fruit, duck eggs, dried shrimp, noodles and general Chinese groceries.

Eldo Cake House

36 Harrison Ave

🚇 Subway to Chinatown

Open: Mon–Sat 0700–1830, Sun 0800–1830

No credit cards accepted

In addition to the beautiful cakes filled either with whipped cream or chestnut cream, Eldo has a great selection of steamed buns for impromptu picnics or lunch on the run. Have a few roast pork or beef buns for a meal, then follow them up with a lotus seed paste turnover.

Mei Tung Oriental Food Supermarket

109 Lincoln St

🚇 Subway to South Station

Open: Sun–Thu 0830–2000, Fri–Sat 0830–2030

Mei Tung, Chinatown's mega-market, attracts ethnic Chinese from a 30-mile radius for their extensive selection of dry goods, canned goods and produce. The butchers' section is among Chinatown's very best.

See Sun Ho Kee

19–25 Harrison Ave

🚇 Subway to Chinatown

Open: Mon–Sat 0800–1800, closed Sun

The selection of canned and dry goods at See Sun Ho Kee is fairly limited, but the choices of hot, cooked meats for takeaways more than compensate for a restricted range of groceries.

Thai Binh Supermarket

15 Beach St, Chinatown

🚇 Subway to Chinatown

Open: Mon–Sat 0800–1800, closed Sun

No credit cards accepted

All Chinatown markets carry some Thai and Vietnamese foods, but Thai Binh strikes nearly a 50–50 balance between Chinese and Southeast Asian groceries and produce in deference to the changing demographics of the neighbourhood.

▲ Instant noodle soups at a Chinatown grocer

Song for your supper

From jamming to jazz

Background music is nearly ubiquitous in Boston restaurants, from the pop radio station at a breakfast café to sophisticated loops of instrumental jazz at some of the hipper chefs' venues. Music sets the mood – and it provides a screen of privacy. Some restaurants go one step further, employing live musicians to turn mealtimes into a night of entertainment.

The accomplished jazz musicians of Berklee College of Music hold forth most nights at **Bob the Chef's Restaurant** (*604 Columbus Ave; ✆ 617-536-6204;* ❸❸), just half a block from Massachusetts Avenue. Right on the line between the hip South End and the historically African-American neighbourhood of Roxbury, Bob the Chef's is a great place to

groove after American soul food. The Sunday jazz brunch is one of the neighbourhood's leading social events.

By booking a table at **Les Zygomates Wine Bar & Bistro** (*see page 42*) in the Leather District near South Station, you'll be sure to see as well as hear the small jazz combos. Walk in off the street, and you might have to settle for a seat in the other room. Either way, Les Zyg has a hearty French bistro menu and a broad choice of wines by the glass.

Jazz and pop fans might also check out the **Lizard Lounge** (*1667 Massachusetts Ave, Cambridge; ✆ 617-547-1228; music Tue–Sat;* ❸). An intimate basement bar with small tables, Lizard Lounge imports the pub grub menu from its upstairs restaurant, the **Cambridge Common**, where pot

▲ House of Blues in Harvard Square

pies and burgers headline the choices. A varying cover charge is levied, and the music rarely starts before 2100.

One of the founders of the Hard Rock Café chain struck out on his own with an outpost for blues purists, **House of Blues** (*96 Winthrop St, Cambridge; ✆ 617-491-2583; music nightly;* ❸❸), in Harvard Square. Now it's a national chain. Some of the promotional showmanship is over the top, but the nightly performances are as solid as a blues beat. You can eat in a separate dining room or order from a more limited menu during the show (varying cover charges). The gospel buffet brunch on Sun (❸❸❸) is such a hit that it's often booked weeks ahead.

Music has become so prominent at the **Middle East** (*472–80 Massachusetts Ave, Central Sq, Cambridge; ✆ 617-492-9181;* ❸❸) that it threatens to overshadow the original bakery-restaurant, where the menu stretches beyond the usual houmous and *shish* kebab to such dishes as pumpkin *kibbeh*. A must on the way up for local and even touring alt-rock bands, the Middle East puts the headliners in the downstairs hall and has newcomers set up in the upstairs bar-cum-dining room. Cover charges vary.

For loud rock and raw fish, no place delivers better than the Back Bay's **Gyuhama** (*827 Boylston St; ✆ 617-437-0188;* ❸❸❸). Boston's oldest Japanese restaurant switches into 'midnight rock 'n' roll sushi' mode every night between 2300 and 0200 with kimono-clad waitresses serving to the throb of mostly local heavy metal rock.

Johnny D's (*17 Holland St, Davis Sq, Somerville; ✆ 617-776-2004;* ❸❸) offers a more mellow combination of music and meal, just two Red Line subway stops beyond Harvard Square. The menu might be called 'healthy bar food', as the kitchen is big on organic ingredients, reduced fat and the like, yet still manages to turn out credible main courses that range from vegetarian bean burritos to steak au poivre and a hefty chocolate fudge layer cake. Music follows dinner, but diners with tickets get to keep their tables for the shows (varying cover charges) of nationally touring blues and acoustic rock and pop acts.

Singer-songwriters still consider **Club Passim** (*see page 83*) one of the holy rites of passage for a recording artist on the way up. This tiny Harvard Square coffee-house with a Middle-Eastern lunch and dinner menu was ground zero in the 1960s folk music boom (Joan Baez and Van Morrison were regulars) and many a plaintive singer hopes lightning will strike again. Make an advance booking for dinner to get one of the best tables for the show (cover varies).

Kimono-clad waitresses serve to the throb of mostly local heavy metal rock.

Back Bay and Fenway

With its grid structure and elegant Victorian architecture, Back Bay overflows with cafés that offer pavement dining as well as a number of top-flight fine dining restaurants. Funkier Fenway (west of Massachusetts Avenue) is home to small and quirky restaurants, plus well-mannered dining at Boston's two major art museums.

BACK BAY AND FENWAY
Restaurants

Anago ❶

Lenox Hotel, 65 Exeter St

⌀ 617-266-6222

🚇 Subway to Copley

Open: brunch Sun 1100–1300; dinner Mon–Sat 1730–2200, Sun 1730–2100

Reservations essential

All credit cards accepted

New American

$$

Chef Bob Calderone synthesises Tuscan, Provençal and American cuisines for a hearty style all his own, making liberal use of an open wood-fired grill for dishes such as spit-roasted pork with apple chutney and roasted root vegetables. The pastries are among the best in the city.

Barcode ❷

955 Boylston St

⌀ 617-421-1818

🚇 Subway to Hynes/ICA

Open: daily 1730–0100

Reservations recommended

All credit cards accepted

New American

$$

Chic and refined, Barcode attracts an upwardly mobile set for sleek, Asian-influenced food such as pan-seared trout with barley risotto, or dumplings filled with butternut squash and crisped in browned butter. The wine list is unusually select and fairly priced, especially for a place where many patrons prefer martinis.

Brasserie Jo ❸

Colonnade Hotel, 120 Huntington Ave

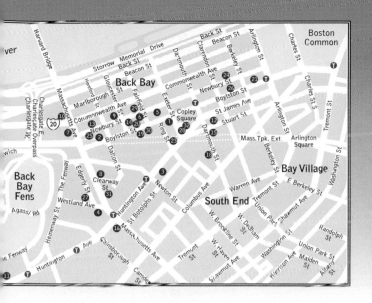

Ø 617-425-3240

🔘 Subway to Prudential

Open: Mon–Fri 0630–2300,
Sat–Sun 0700–2300

Reservations recommended

VISA AMERICAN EXPRESS

French

💲💲💲

The brasserie food
(steak-*frites*, baked
salmon, *tarte Tatin*) can
be uneven and the ser-
vice is sometimes *too*
French, but Jo is popular
for socialising over kir
and pâté or sausages
and Alsatian beer.

Brown Rice ④

14A Westland Ave

Ø 617-247-5320

🔘 Subway to Symphony

Open: daily 1130–1300,
1700–2230

Reservations unnecessary

VISA AMERICAN EXPRESS

Thai

💲💲

Around the corner from
Symphony Hall, Brown
Rice is a good spot to
dine before a concert.
The light and healthy
food won't make you
drift off listening to

Brahms. Both grilled
and steamed salmon are
house specialities, while
the more adventurous
might prefer the duck
with fiery Thai curry.
True to the name, rice
and noodles are whole-
grain versions.

Chanterelle ⑤

226 Newbury St

Ø 617-262-8988

▲ Outdoor dining at Ciao Bella

 Subway to Copley

Open: Mon–Tue, Sat–Sun 1730–2400, Wed–Fri 1730–0100

Reservations recommended

All credit cards accepted

French

💲💲

Newbury St's below-ground bistro evokes a bygone era when Americans thought owning a beret and listening to Edith Piaf were terribly romantic. No gastronomic ground is broken with the likes of vegetable *potage* or chicken with mushrooms and crêpes, but it's soothing food in a genteel setting – ideal on a cool, rainy day.

Ciao Bella 6

240 Newbury St

∅ 617-536-2626

 Subway to Copley

Open: Sun–Wed 1130–2300, Thu–Sat 1130–2330

Reservations recommended

All credit cards accepted

Italian

💲💲

This is strictly retro Italian from the minestrone soup through to the chicken *parmigiano*. But the food isn't the point: Most people come to sit at outdoor tables at this trendy corner of Newbury and Fairfield to see and be seen among visiting sports stars and celebrities.

Clio 7

Eliot Hotel, 370 Commonwealth Ave

∅ 617-536-7200

 Subway to Auditorium

Open: Sun and Tue–Thu 1730–2200, Fri 1730–2230, Sat 1500–2230, closed Mon

Reservations essential

All credit cards accepted

New American

💲💲💲

One of Boston's temples of haute cuisine, Clio matches a quietly elegant dining room with exuberantly colourful and carefully constructed plates. Probably the only place in town likely to offer a swordfish steak au poivre with vegetables such as purple *kohlrabi* on the side, Clio also has a wine list worthy of a baron and an 11-course tasting menu available every night.

Dixie Kitchen 8

182 Massachusetts Ave

∅ 617-536-3068

 Subway to Hynes/ICA

Open: daily 1100–2300

Reservations not allowed

 American Express

Cajun

💲

The 'cooking with jazz' neon sign signals that the style is more New Orleans than Nashville, with a mean fried catfish, low-key jambalaya and a pretty passable shrimp *étouffé*. The Christian Science church is the landlord, so the long-necked bottles of beer usually associated with this cuisine are simply unavailable. The 'seafood jazz combo' is a great plate of fried cat-fish, shrimp and oysters.

L'Espalier

30 Gloucester St

Ø 617-262-3023

Subway to Copley or Hynes/ICA

Open: Mon–Sat 1800–2200, closed Sun

Reservations essential

All credit cards accepted

French-New American

There's at least a marriage proposal per week at L'Espalier. Set in a gracious town-house, lit by flickering candles and staffed by impeccable waiters and brilliant cooks, L'Espalier would make Escoffier proud. Chef-owner Frank McClelland's vegetarian main courses are every bit as complex as those with meat. Bring a good supply of credit cards for the *prix fixe* dining experience of a lifetime.

Himalaya

95 Massachusetts Ave

Ø 617-267-6644

Subway to Hynes/ICA

Open: Sun–Thu 1100–2300, Fri–Sat 1100–2400

Reservations unnecessary

All credit cards accepted

Indian

The name suggests the northerly segment of the Indian subcontinent and, true to form, meats from the tandoori oven feature prominently on the menu. But Himalaya really shines with the spicy dishes of the west coast and the aromatic concoctions of the south. The luncheon buffet is a great deal.

Museum of Fine Arts Restaurant

465 Huntington Ave

Ø 617-369-3474

Subway to Museum

Open: lunch Mon–Sat 1130–1430, Sun 1100–1500; dinner Wed–Fri 1730–2030

Reservations recommended

All credit cards accepted

New American

The menu matches the airy modernity of the museum's West Wing with dishes that empha-sise local produce and fish. Expect such delights as saffron *fet-tucine* with pieces of lobster sautéed in butter.

▲ Oak Room

▲ Oyster Bar at Turner Fisheries

Oak Room 🄬

Fairmont Copley Plaza
Hotel, 138 St James Ave

✆ 617-267-5300

🚇 Subway to Copley

Open: Sun–Thu 1730–2200,
Fri–Sat 1730–2300

Reservations essential

All credit cards accepted

American

❸❸❸

With stunning baroque
woodwork and carved
ceilings, the Oak Room
is a Boston classic for
perfectly grilled,
massive slabs of meat
and fish along with icy
martinis and such retro
classics as oysters
Rockefeller.

Sonsie 🄭

327 Newbury St

✆ 617-351-2500

🚇 Subway to Hynes/ICA

Open: daily 0700–0100

Reservations recommended

All credit cards accepted

American

❸❸

A gorgeous spot for
breakfast with the sun
streaming in, Sonsie
swings back the huge
glass doors in warm
weather, though
wrenching an outdoor
table away from cigar-
smoking poseurs can be
tricky. Too bad, because
the food can be very
tasty and inventive.

Tapeo 🄮

268 Newbury St

✆ 617-267-4799

🚇 Subway to Copley or
Hynes/ICA

Open: Mon–Wed 1700–
2230, Thu–Fri 1700–2330,
Sat 1200–2330, Sun 1200–
2230

Reservations recommended

All credit cards accepted

Spanish

❸

Tapas and Spanish
sparkling wine make the
perfect light meal at
outdoor café tables.
Watch the human
parade and munch

serrano ham, Manchego
cheese, garlicky prawns
and slices of cold
Spanish omelette.

Turner Fisheries 🄯

Westin Hotel, Dartmouth
and Stuart Sts

✆ 617-424-7425

🚇 Subway to Back Bay or
Copley

Open: lunch Mon–Fri 1130–
1430; brunch Sat 1130–
1500, Sun 1030–1430;
dinner 1730–2230

All credit cards accepted

Seafood

❸❸❸

For an elegant room
with a menu tied to the
day's fish auction,
Turner has no Boston
peers. The delicious
clam chowder domi-
nates local tasting
competitions.

Betty's Wok & Noodle Diner 16

250 Huntington Ave

🚇 Subway to Symphony

Open: Mon–Sat 1130–2300, Sun 1130–2200

💳 🈂 American Express

Pick a rice or noodle, chicken or vegetable and a sauce at this tongue-in-cheek, design-your-own-dinner spot decorated in 1950s-chic. Good salads and hefty, traditional American desserts (eg, chocolate layer cake) round off the experience.

Gardner Museum Café 17

280 The Fenway

🚇 Subway to Museum

Open: Tue–Fri 1130–1600, Sat–Sun 1100–1600, closed Mon

💳 🈂 American Express

Just a tiny pocket of the museum mansion, the café expands into a

garden deck in warm weather. It's a fine spot for tea, lobster bisque or a smoked salmon club sandwich (lox, dill and egg salad).

Hazel's Country Kitchen 18

130 Dartmouth St

🚇 Subway to Back Bay

Open: Mon–Fri 0700–2300, Sat–Sun 0800–2300

🈂 💳 American Express

Hazel's infuses flair into traditional country cooking – cornmeal-crusted chicken with roasted potatoes, salmon smothered in pesto, and excellent, smoky Texas beef ribs. Moreover, they serve breakfast all day.

Marché Mövenpick 19

Prudential Center, 800 Boylston St

🚇 Subway to Hynes/ICA or Prudential

Open: daily 0730–0200

All credit cards accepted

If you like having a dozen chain restaurants under one roof, Marché issues a 'passport' that is stamped at each themed station where you choose food that could range from pasta to sweet and sour pork to roast beef. It's perfect for family groups where everyone wants something different.

New England Soup Factory 20

855 Boylston St

🚇 Subway to Hynes/ICA

Open: Mon–Fri 0700–1900, Sat–Sun 1100–1900

💳 🈂

Great soup is a meal in a bowl, especially with crusty rolls on the side. Chicken vegetable soup and clam and lobster chowders are always available, with a rotating selection of four other choices as well as salads and sandwiches. Everything can be packed for takeaways.

Parish Café 21

361 Boylston St

🚇 Subway to Arlington

Open: Mon–Sat 1130–0100, Sun 1200–0100

All credit cards accepted

Main courses such as meatloaf and fish cakes

▲ Dining al fresco on Newbury Street

are good comfort food, but the real treats at the Parish Café are sandwiches designed by several of the city's top chefs – Lydia Shire's lobster salad on pepper brioche, for example, or Jody Adams' *prosciutto* and fresh mozzarella on white bread.

El Pelón Taquería ㉒

92 Peterborough St

🚇 Subway to Fenway

Open: Tue–Sun 1130–2230, closed Mon

No credit cards accepted

El Pelón serves inventive, authentic Mexican fare at rock-bottom prices, at the edge of the Back Bay Fens not far from the Museum of Fine Arts. Thick, meaty plantains are grilled perfectly, as is the *mako* shark in a filled house speciality taco.

Tennessee's Barbecue ㉓

47 Huntington Ave

🚇 Subway to Copley

Open: daily 1100–2100

All credit cards accepted

With some of the best Texan-style barbecued beef ribs in Boston and a fabulous pulled (shredded) pork plate, Tennessee's is a find. Seating is extremely limited, but everything can be taken away.

Torrefazione Italia ㉔

85 Newbury St

🚇 Subway to Arlington or Copley

Open: Mon–Fri 0700–2100, Sat 0800–2100, Sun 0900–2100

Stunning coffee tastes even better in bright Italian crockery. Vegetarians fare well with sandwich combos such as feta cheese,

roasted peppers, mixed greens and crumbled blue cheese on *focaccia*.

Trident Booksellers Café ㉕

338 Newbury St

🚇 Subway to Hynes/ICA

Open: daily 0900–2330

All credit cards accepted

With a pleasant ambience of books, magazines and contemporary music, Trident favours student café fare but also serves wine and beer.

White Star Tavern ㉖

565 Boylston St

🚇 Subway to Arlington or Copley

Open: Mon 1700–2400, Tue–Fri 1130–2400, Sat–Sun 1100–2400

All credit cards accepted

Good light eats range from shrimp *tempura* to *penne* with lobster and Tasso ham to terrific fish and chips.

BACK BAY AND FENWAY
Shops, markets and picnic sites

Shops

Bread & Circus 🄧

15 Westland St

🚇 Subway to Symphony

Open: daily 0900–2200

🈯 💳 American Express
Discover

Natural foods, exquisite produce, salads and sandwiches are a boon to frugal travellers, despite the slightly high prices. Cheese selection rivals a good Parisian *fromagerie*.

De Luca's Market 🄩

239 Newbury St

🚇 Subway to Copley

Open: Mon–Sat 0700–2200, Sun 0700–2100

🈯 💳 American Express

This branch of De Luca's is smaller than the Charles St edition, but stocks top-grade fruits and vegetables as well as deli meats and other conveniences. The polish on the apples and the convenience add a bit to the price, but goods are top quality.

Star Market 🄪

800 Boylston St

🚇 Subway to Copley

Open: 24 hours a day, closed Sun 2400–0700

🈯 💳 American Express
Discover

An outpost of one of Boston's oldest chain grocers, this Star branch has a mind-boggling selection of canned and packaged goods. The deli sells sliced meats and cheeses and also salads, soups and sandwiches for takeaways.

Markets

Copley Square Farmers' Market 🄫

St. James Ave, Copley Sq

🚇 Subway to Copley

Open: June–mid-Oct Tue and Fri 1100–1800

No credit cards accepted

Area farmers bring freshly picked vegetables, fruits and flowers to this small public market twice weekly. Look for strawberries and raspberries in June and July, blueberries and peaches in August and pears and apples thereafter.

Picnic sites

Christian Science Center 🄬

Massachusetts Ave at Huntington Ave

🚇 Subway to Symphony

The Massachusetts Avenue side of the world headquarters of the First Church of Christ, Scientist, offers broad green lawns to spread out a repast. The reflecting pool on the Huntington Avenue side lacks the grass but offers the soothing sound of running water and elegant modern architecture.

Copley Square 🄴

Bounded by Clarendon St, Dartmouth St, Boylston St and St James Ave

🚇 Subway to Copley

An ideal spot to loll in the grass surrounded by landmark architecture, Copley Square also has plenty of benches for sitting in the sun while consuming a sandwich.

▲ Picnicking on the lawn of the Christian Science Center

Rooms with a view

Feasts for the eyes

When it came to rooms with a view, restaurateurs used to figure they could substitute a feast for the eyes with good food on the plate. But these days Bostonians are lucky to have a number of places to dine where the scene and the meal usually converge in aesthetic harmony. Alas, even rooms that accept advance bookings will only rarely guarantee the best tables with unobstructed views. Early-bird diners often get the pick of the seats.

Relatively low-rise Boston has just two skyscraper restaurants. The **Top of the Hub Restaurant** (*Prudential Center, 800 Boylston St; ✆ 617-536-1775; booking recommended;* ❸❸❸) towers high above Back Bay, offering long views of Boston's 19th-century red-brick neighbourhoods and the snaking blue ribbon of the Charles River. West-facing tables are the city's best sunset perches.

The **Bay Tower** (*see page 29*) sits closer to the waterfront. Boston's first capital investors had headquarters on this spot to keep an eye on their ships in the harbour. The Bay Tower has that same eagle-eye view – but from 33 storeys above State Street, where the entire 30-mile length of Boston harbour is visible.

Those million-dollar views come at a price, but diners can get in on the ground floor by frequenting eateries on the shoreline. Cafés and restaurants have sprung up like artists gentrifying a warehouse district as Boston has reclaimed and spruced up its once-rundown docks.

Joe's American Bar & Grill (*100 Atlantic Ave; ✆ 617-367-*

▲ Boston harbour

8700; ❻❻) occupies a prime waterside spot barely on the North End side of Christopher Columbus Park. Although the outdoor tables are appealing, the indoor tables along a glass wall have the most intimate harbour views. Practically next door, the smaller **Boston Sail Loft Restaurant** (*80 Atlantic Ave; ✆ 617-227-7280;* ❻❻) is particularly popular with the topsider-shod members of the Boston Sailing Center. **Intrigue** (*Boston Harbor Hotel, 70 Rowes Wharf; ✆ 617-856-7744;* ❻❻) is the casual restaurant of the Boston Harbor Hotel.

The Boston shoreline bends at Fort Point Channel, so the South Boston side of the channel looks back on the inner harbour and the city skyline. **Barking Crab** (*see page 22*) sits literally on the channel's bank, facing over the water to the glass menagerie of Financial District towers. The view from **Sebastian's Café** (*see page 23*) in the US Courthouse graces virtually every magazine article or guidebook about the city.

Most waterfront tables look from the city to the harbour, but to turn the tables, book one of the **Odyssey Cruises** (*Rowes Wharf; ✆ 617-654-9700;* ❻❻❻). They operate daily in summer, less often in winter. During high season, options include a Sunday brunch cruise, lunch cruises from Monday to Saturday, and a nightly dinner cruise. The night

▲ Enjoying a meal at Café Ravello in the North End

view of Boston as the ship returns to berth is the icing on the cake – better than the dessert.

Because the banks of the Charles River are lined with parkland, Boston's 'other' waterfront has more picnic spots than restaurants. But there are a few prime lookouts near the mouth of the river. Tables at **Davio's** (*5 Cambridge Parkway, Cambridge; ✆ 617-661-4810;* ❻❻❻) in the Royal Sonesta Hotel gaze out across the Charles River to the skylines of Beacon Hill and Back Bay. The best view of the river itself is from the family-friendly food court at the **Museum of Science** (*Science Park, ✆ 617-723-2500;* ❻), which actually sits atop a dam on the Charles River.

Sometimes striking views materialise in some of the least likely places. From the large windows of the second-floor dining room of **Café Ravello** (*48 Salem St; ✆ 617-723-5182;* ❻❻) in the North End, Boston truly appears as a 'city-on-a-hill'.

> **Two skyscraper restaurants tower above Back Bay, offering long views of Boston's 19th-century red-brick neighbourhoods and the snaking blue ribbon of the Charles River.**

South End

This gracious 19th-century red-brick neighbourhood declined into tenements before rebounding with recent renovation. One of the most ethnically diverse parts of the city, the South End also hosts a lively gay culture and an unusual number of visual and performing artists. A sure sign of the renaissance is the explosion in fine cafés and restaurants. Most visitors tend to spend their time in the South End on Columbus Avenue and Tremont Street near the Boston Center for the Arts.

SOUTH END
Restaurants

Aquitaine ❶

569 Tremont St

✆ 617-424-8577

Ⓣ Subway to Back Bay

Open: dinner Sun–Wed 1730–2300, Thu–Sat 1730–2400; brunch Sat–Sun 1000–1400

Reservations essential

VISA ● American Express

French

❸❸❸

This ambitious Parisian-style bistro lightens up on the traditional cream-and-butter style, with *plats du jour* ranging from *cassoulet* and *choucroute* to *bouillabaisse*. The extensive wine selection, mostly French, is displayed on the walls as part of the smart décor.

Dish ❸

253 Shawmut Ave

✆ 617-426-7866

Ⓣ Subway to Back Bay

Open: dinner 1700–2400; Sun brunch 1100–1500

Reservations not allowed

VISA ● American Express

New American

❸❸

Small, friendly and reasonably priced, Dish could make you wish you lived in the neighbourhood so you could eat here nightly, alternating between tasty meals such as grilled vegetables on a thin, crispy whole-wheat pizza crust or wood-oven-roasted chicken marinated in thyme, honey and lemon.

Giacomo's ❹

431 Columbus Ave

✆ 617-536-5723

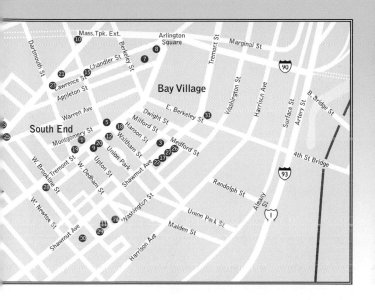

Ⓢ Subway to Massachusetts Ave

Open: Tue–Thu 1730–2200, Fri–Sat 1700–2300, Sun 1700–2200

Reservations recommended

No credit cards accepted

Italian

⑤⑤

Giacomo's is known for its pastas, such as butternut squash ravioli, and its fish dishes. A good choice is the *zuppa di pesce* for two – lobster, clams and other shellfish heaped over a bowl of *linguine*.

Hamersley's Bistro ⑤

553 Tremont St

Ø 617-423-2700

▲ Front bar at Aquitaine

▲ Chris Douglass of Icarus chopping leeks

🜃 Subway to Back Bay

Open: Mon–Fri 1800–2200, Sat 1730–2230, Sun 1730–2130

Reservations essential

All credit cards accepted

French-New American

❸❸❸

Gordon Hamersley is among Boston's great chefs, and his signature dish is Boston's best roast chicken. The entire French provincial menu is simultaneously simple and sophisticated, rustic and refined. Desserts are satisfyingly rich, such as triple *pots de crème* (maple, chocolate and raspberry).

House of Siam ❻

542 Columbus Ave

✆ 617-267-1755

🜃 Subway to Massachusetts Ave

Open: Mon–Thu 1130–2200, Fri 1130–2300, Sat 1200–2300, Sun 1200–2200

Reservations recommended

All credit cards accepted

Thai-Malaysian

❸❸

House of Siam excels in Malay curries as well as such Thai standbys as *pad Thai*. Its international outlook means that spicing tends to be subtle rather than fiery or perfumed.

Icarus ❼

3 Appleton St

✆ 617-426-1790

🜃 Subway to Back Bay

Open: Mon–Thu 1800–2130,
Fri 1800–2200, Sat 1730–
2230, Sun 1730–2100

Reservations recommended

All credit cards accepted

New American

❸❸❸

Icarus is a time-
honoured romantic
haunt and chef Chris
Douglass is a champion
of New American
cooking. Expect the
unexpected, such as
venison with pomegran-
ates and wild-rice
pancakes.

Masa ❽

439 Tremont St

✆ 617-338-8884

Ⓢ Subway to Back Bay

Open: Tue–Thu, Sun 1700–
2200, Fri–Sat 1700–2300,
closed Mon

Reservations recommended

America American Express
Discover

New American

❸❸❸

Masa applies southwest-
ern accents to New
England fare with great
effect in such dishes as
pan-roasted cod with
smoked pepper bacon
served with a sauce of
charred tomatoes and
sweet corn. The bar
makes a killer margarita.

Metropolis Café ❾

584 Tremont St

✆ 617-247-2931

Ⓢ Subway to Back Bay

Open: Mon–Wed, Sun 1730–
2200, Thu–Sat 1730–2300;
brunch Sat–Sun 0900 1500

Reservations essential

America American Express

New American-Italian

❸❸❸

Tiny and incredibly
chic, Metropolis focuses
on seafood with such
dishes as mussels in
saffron broth or striped
bass in a rich pinot noir
sauce. The risotto
changes daily but is
always a good choice.

Mistral ❿

223 Columbus Ave

✆ 617-867-9300

Ⓢ Subway to Back Bay

Open: Sun and Tue–Thu
1730–2400, Fri–Sat 1730
2445, closed Mon

Reservations essential

All credit cards accepted

New American

❸❸❸

Chef Jamie Mammano
serves picture-perfect
bistro fare (eg, grilled
rib-eye steak with
horseradish whipped
potatoes) in drop-dead
designer surroundings.

Pho République ⓫

1415 Washington St

✆ 617-262-0005

Ⓢ Subway to Back Bay

Open: daily 1730–0100

Reservations not allowed

America American

French-Vietnamese-New
American

❸❸

French colonial and
Vietnamese cuisines get
a tweak of urbane
American sass at Pho
République. The *pho*
(soups) come in vege-
tarian as well as duck,
chicken, shrimp, beef or

smoked pork versions in
one of the least expen-
sive ultra-hip dining
rooms in Boston.

South End
Galleria ❷

480 Columbus Ave

✆ 617-236-5252

Ⓢ Subway to Mass Ave or
Back Bay

Open: daily 1730–2400

Reservations recommended

America American Express

New American-Italian

❸❸

Poets, jazz mavens and
conceptual artists meet
at this spot designed to
resemble a Roman alley
café. With Abruzzi
owners and a keen eye
for fickle neighbour-
hood tastes, La Bettola
is a great place to enjoy
Mediterranean-
influenced bistro fare
and drink with South
End hipsters.

Truc ⓬

560 Tremont St

✆ 617-338-8070

Ⓢ Subway to Back Bay

Open: Tue–Sat 1800–2200,
Sun 1800–2100, closed Mon

Reservations recommended

America Discover

French

❸❸❸

Truc hones in on hearty,
simple French bistro
fare (coq au vin, beet-
and-*mâché* salad, crème
brûlée) with satisfying
success. The wine list is
exquisite, if complex.

SOUTH END
Bars, cafés and pubs

Charlie's Sandwich Shop ⑬

429 Columbus Ave

Ⓢ Subway to Massachusetts Ave

Open: Mon–Fri 0600–1430, Sat 0730–1300, closed Sun

No credit cards accepted

This working-class all-day diner established in 1927 is acclaimed for its meatloaf and its turkey hash, which might explain the crowds spilling out of the doors at around noon each day.

Claremont Café ⑭

535 Columbus Ave

Ⓢ Subway to Massachusetts Ave

Open: breakfast Tue–Fri 0730–1130; lunch Tue–Fri 1130–1500; dinner Tue–Thu 1730–2200, Fri–Sat 1730–2230; brunch Sat 0800–1500, Sun 0900–1500

🔲 🔷 American Express

You could happily eat all your meals at this American bistro with influences from Latin America and the Mediterranean, starting with a goats' cheese frittata in the morning, sweet potato polenta for lunch and luscious braised lamb shank with lentils and cucumber salad at night.

Delux Café ⑮

100 Chandler St

Ⓢ Subway to Back Bay

Open: Mon–Sat 1700–2330, closed Sun

No credit cards accepted

Prices are rock bottom at this funky New American kitchen with such dishes as catfish and hush puppies and smoky seafood *cioppino*.

Everyday Café ⑯

517 Columbus Ave

Ⓢ Subway to Massachusetts Ave

Open: Mon and Wed–Fri 0700–1900, Sat 0900–1900, Sun 0900–1700, closed Tue

🔲 🔷

▲ Hanging out at the Kettle Café

Stunning Greek salads and oregano-laced sandwiches are the highlights at this ultra-casual vegetarian café that also has breads and some groceries for take-aways. Blended drinks of milk, fruit and yoghurt (called 'smoothies') are also very popular.

Franklin Café ⑰

278 Shawmut Ave

Ⓢ Subway to Back Bay

Open: daily 1730–0130

VISA 💳 American Express

Franklin Café looks like a big boxy bar, but the dinners served in the wooden booths reveal it to be an imaginative bistro at heart, with such dishes as ground-turkey meatloaf smothered in earthy fig gravy. Arrive early at weekends, as they don't allow advance bookings and the Franklin is a big hit with the neighbourhood residents.

Le Gamin ⑱

550 Tremont St

Ⓢ Subway to Back Bay

Open: Mon–Fri 1000–2400, Sat–Sun 0800–2400

VISA 💳

Essentially a lace-curtained French crêperie with superb savoury and sweet options for every meal, Le Gamin also makes good crustless quiche and sandwiches piled high on crispy breads. This stylish spot is right opposite the Boston Center for the Arts.

Garden of Eden Café ⑲

571 Tremont St

Ⓢ Subway to Back Bay

Open: Sun 0730–2300, Mon–Thu 0730–2300, Fri–Sat 0700–0100

VISA 💳 American Express

Elegant sandwiches, exquisite desserts and a broad selection of imported and domestic cheeses and pâtés are available to consume at café tables or to take away for a deluxe picnic.

Geoffrey's Café-Bar ⑳

578 Tremont St

Ⓢ Subway to Back Bay

Open: Sun–Thu 0900–2230, Fri–Sat 0900–2300

VISA 💳 American Express

There's a real discrepancy between Geoffrey's hard-edge wine-bar décor and its soothing comfort food, which ranges from eggs Benedict at breakfast and generous deli sandwiches at lunch to flank steak marinated in zesty citrus juices and tangy garlic in the evening.

Kettle Café ㉑

288 Columbus Ave

Ⓢ Subway to Back Bay

Open: Mon–Fri 0700–1500, Sat 0800–1700, closed Sun

No credit cards accepted

This neighbourhood coffee shop serves excellent sandwiches (turkey, Manchego cheese and tomato on spinach and walnut bread) and soothing soups as well as coffee. Linger over a latte and one of the free newspapers while munching a lime and sugar cane cookie.

The Purple Cactus Burrito & Wrap Bar ㉒

312 Shawmut Ave

Ⓢ Subway to Back Bay

Open: daily 1130–2200

VISA 💳

'Wraps' outnumber burritos by far, making this more Californian than Mexican, but the fillings are tasty and many are vegetarian. The tiny storefront is a good stop for quick, fresh and healthy hand-held meals.

Shops

Aguadilla Market ㉘

664 Tremont St

🚇 Subway to Back Bay

Open: daily 0800–1800

No credit cards accepted

Adjacent to the principally Puerto Rican Villa Victoria housing complex, this small market specialises in Latin American and Caribbean staples and produce, such as guavas and yucca.

Bakery at Haley House ㉓

23 Dartmouth St

🚇 Subway to Back Bay

Open: Mon 0630–0930, Tue–Fri 0630–0930, 1430–1930, Sat–Sun 0630–0730

No credit cards accepted

Haley House is a soup kitchen for the indigent and elderly, and its bakery serves as a neighbourhood skill-training program. It's a great place to purchase breads, pies, brownies and muffins and specialises in kosher produce.

Foodie's Urban Market ㉙

1421–23 Washington St

🚇 Subway to Back Bay

Open: Mon–Sat 0800–2100, Sun 0900–2000

💳 💳 American Express Discover

Natural foods, excellent produce, and a vast selection of canned and

packaged goods make Foodie's the largest, most comprehensive market in the South End.

Morse Fish Company ㉔

1401 Washington St

🚇 Subway to Back Bay

Open: Mon–Fri 1000–2000, Sat 1000–2000, closed Sun

💳 💳 American Express

Directly across from Holy Cross Cathedral, Morse has the day's catch on crushed ice in handsome cases. The takeaway counter also sells bargain fish dinners.

New Boston Wine & Spirits Center ㉕

474 Columbus Ave

🚇 Subway to Back Bay

Open: Mon–Sat 0900–2245, closed Sun

💳 💳 American Express Discover

New Boston groups wines from around the world by drinking style (eg, 'light whites for seafood'). With fair prices and a broad selection of mid-range bottles, New Boston outshines the neighbourhood's other wine shops.

South End Formaggio ㉖

268 Shawmut Ave

🚇 Subway to Back Bay

Open: Mon–Fri 0900–2000, Sat 0900–1900, Sun 1100–1700

💳 💳 American Express

This outlet for the famed Cambridge cheese importer carries up to 250 cheeses from Europe and North America, many of them aged to perfection in a custom cellar before being released for sale. Hot soups, sandwiches and baked goods are also available.

Syrian Grocery Importing Company ㉗

270 Shawmut Ave

🚇 Subway to Back Bay

Open: Tue–Sat 1100–1830, closed Sun–Mon

No credit cards accepted

The South End has a long history of immigration from the Middle East (Lebanese poet and philosopher Khalil Gibran grew up here) and this shop has been bringing foods from the homeland for generations. It's the place to find grape leaves, ground *sumack* or *za'atar*.

Picnic sites

Blackstone Square ㉚

Between Shawmut Ave and Washington St at West Brookline St

🚇 Subway to Back Bay

With its circular fountain surrounded by wooden-slatted cast-iron benches, Blackstone Square (and its mirror image on the other side of Washington St, Franklin Square) can be a serene spot to settle in with a sandwich and let

the sun beat down on your face.

Peters Park ㉛

Between Washington St and Shawmut Ave at East Berkeley St

🚇 Subway to Back Bay

Near Holy Cross Cathedral, Peters Park is an active space with a baseball field, soccer ground and basketball and tennis courts. But there's also a periphery of welcoming green lawns for spreading a blanket to enjoy a picnic.

Southwest Corridor Park ㉜

West of Columbus Ave from Back Bay Station to Roxbury

🚇 Subway to Back Bay or Massachusetts Ave

This corridor park links together green cul-de-sacs on the western edge of the South End. Primarily used as a bicycling and in-line skating park, it has many pleasant green spaces for picnicking.

Sparrow Park ㉝

Behind Union Church (485 Columbus Ave) between West Rutland and West Newton Sts

🚇 Subway to Back Bay or Massachusetts Ave

This serene set-aside behind the South End's Gothic Revival-style Methodist Church is full of benches, making it a popular place to eat lunch in warm weather.

Best bets for brunch

An all-American tradition

The classic restorative on the morning after the night before, brunch has become almost a standard Sunday meal in Boston as diners linger with the *Boston Globe* and the *New York Times*, reading each other odd bits from the social pages or the book reviews. Scattered family members or groups of friends often congregate for brunch because the meal lends itself to casual conviviality at a more moderate price than dinner. Of course, brunch also serves as a practical combination of breakfast and lunch for late risers or starry-eyed couples concluding an all-night date.

The **Café Fleuri** (*Hotel Meridien, 250 Franklin St; ☎ 617-451-1900; Sun;*

booking essential; ❸❸❸) stages the *ne plus ultra* of buffet brunches. The bounty verges on an embarrassment of riches: hot main courses and a carvery, a table of cold salads and pâtés, a crêpe station and a selection of desserts that makes the display cases of most good bakeries look paltry.

The **Blue Room** (*One Kendall Sq, Cambridge; ☎ 617-494-9034; Sun; booking recommended;* ❸❸) has live jazz combos and a buffet of imaginative small dishes. Meats and fish – seasoned with Moroccan spices, perhaps – stream off a wood grill next to the buffet. Chef Steve Johnson is a passionate advocate of local agriculture and exploits the best market ingredients available.

If you'd prefer that the buffet came to you rather than the other way around, consider *dim sum* in Chinatown at the **China Pearl** (*9 Tyler St; ☎ 617-426-4338;* ❸). The dual red-pink-gold dining rooms fill up at weekends, though China Pearl offers *dim sum* daily from 0830 to 1500. As many as 60 different morsels come rolling past during the noontime peak.

Many restaurants have abandoned the buffet brunch in

favour of an à la carte menu. One of the best is at **Up Stairs at the Pudding** (see page 81). The selections change frequently, but the menu mixes egg dishes (eg, a leek and *crimini* mushroom frittata), meat and fish main courses (a small *filet mignon* with fried eggs and hollandaise sauce) and sweet dishes (apple and cinnamon Belgian waffles with strawberries and brown sugar cream). During warm weather, ask for a table in the outdoor rooftop garden.

A few blocks away, **East Coast Grill** (1271 Cambridge St, Inman Sq, Cambridge; ✆ 617-491-6568; Sun; ●) offers a New American take on Latin American tradition. Hungry diners can dig into a Yucatecan platter with three eggs, black beans and rice; a salad of mango, avocado and hearts of palm; and a dessert of fried plantains. Tortillas stuffed with smoked duck and jack cheese better suit a more modest appetite.

The Hampshire House (84 Beacon St; ✆ 617-227-9600; Sun; booking essential; ●●●) looks out on to the Public Garden, and an elegant jazz combo accompanies a classic brunch with a selection of rich egg dishes. It's the only meal for which this restaurant, usually reserved for private parties and catered affairs, opens to the public.

> **Hungry diners dig into a Yucatecan platter with three eggs, black beans and rice; a salad of mango, avocado and hearts of palm; and a dessert of fried plantains.**

Laurel (142 Berkeley St; ✆ 617-424-6664; ●) prepares a more modest version of traditional brunch dishes, including a hash of roasted chicken, duck and sweet potatoes as well as intriguing versions of French toast and pancakes.

The South End abounds with brunch spots. For one of the more innovative brunches at a leading bistro (dishes might include Thai pea tendril and chicken salad), try **Tremont 647** (647 Tremont St; ✆ 617-266-4600; Sun; advance booking suggested; ●). If you're more of a breakfast person, there's no surpassing the ultra-casual **Mike's City Diner** (1714 Washington St; ✆ 617-267-9393; daily 0600-1500; ●). The Emergency Room Special (Boston City Hospital is nearby) includes two eggs, two pancakes, three pieces of bacon or sausage, fried potatoes or grits and toast for a price low enough to make you blush.

Many Boston Irish pubs offer weekend breakfasts, often accompanied by live music. **Hennessy's of Boston** (25 Union St; ✆ 617-742-2121; ●), for example, features a traditional carvery, while the **Kinsale Irish Pub & Restaurant** (see page 30) serves up a full Irish breakfast of fried eggs, bacon rashers, grilled tomato, baked beans, sautéed mushrooms and black and white puddings.

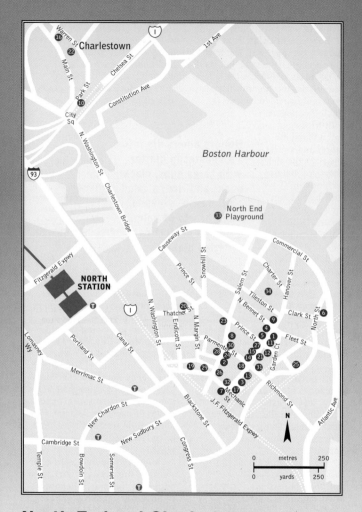

North End and Charlestown

Boston's oldest residential neighbourhood (since 1631), the largely
Italian North End abounds with small cafés, restaurants, trattorias,
bakeries and grocers. The southern Italian cuisine that used to predomi-
nate is being increasingly challenged by innovative young chefs cooking
New American-style food with an Italian accent.

NORTH END AND CHARLESTOWN
Restaurants

Alloro Restaurant ❶

351 Hanover St

☎ 617-523-9268

🚇 Subway to Haymarket

Open: Tue–Thu 1700–2200, Fri–Sat 1130–2300, Sun 1130–2200, closed Mon

Reservations recommended

All credit cards accepted

Italian

💲💲

Alloro has all the finesse that its neighbouring pasta houses lack – intimate tables, attentive service and dishes that combine a multitude of flavours. Typical plates include a shrimp and pungent fennel salad, and the hearty soup of shrimp, mussels, clams and fish in a tomato broth.

Antico Forno ❷

93 Salem St

☎ 617 723-6733

🚇 Subway to Haymarket

Open: lunch 1100–1400; dinner 1700–2200

Reservations recommended

Italian

💲💲

Chef-owner Mario Nocera balances southern Italian simplicity and urban sophistication with baked pastas and brick-oven-seared meats. The breads are heavenly and great for sopping up such delicious sauces as the garlic-wine broth served with roasted shrimp and squid.

Bricco ❸

241 Hanover St

☎ 617-248-6800

🚇 Subway to Haymarket

Open: Tue–Thu 1700–2200, Fri–Sat 1700–2400, closed Sun–Mon

Reservations recommended

All credit cards accepted

Italian-New American

💲💲💲

Like a jazz saxophonist exploring a pop tune, Bricco finds new subtleties of texture and taste in traditional Italian cooking, adding the flavour of smoked red pepper and bitter braised *rabe* to sweet steamed mussels, for example. Room for dessert? Try the chocolate box filled with cookies.

Cantina Italiana ❹

346 Hanover St

☎ 617-723-4577

🚇 Subway to Haymarket

Open: Mon–Sat 1600–2300, Sun 1200–2230

Reservations recommended

All credit cards accepted

Italian

💲💲

Neither the music nor the menu has changed much at Cantina Italiana since Frank Sinatra was a skinny kid singer. Best bets are the old-fashioned southern Italian veal dishes and pastas smothered with tomatoes. The bread and wine can be disappointing.

Cibo ❺

326 Hanover St

☎ 617-557-9248

🚇 Subway to Haymarket

Open: Tue–Thu 1700–2200, Fri 1700–2300, Sat 1130–2300, Sun 1400–2100, closed Mon

Reservations recommended

Italian

💲💲

Cibo brings artful presentation to traditional chicken and veal *marsala, puttanesca, piccata, saltimbocca* ... Occasional unconventional items such as pan-fried Italian greens on crunchy polenta are terrific. Quality takes time, and the kitchen can be slow.

Davide Restaurant ❻

326 Commercial St

☎ 617-227-5745

🚇 Subway to Haymarket

Open: daily 1700–2300

▲ Making pizza in North End

Reservations recommended

Italian

●●●

With red leather upholstery, tuxedoed waiters and busboys (table-clearers) in waistcoats, Davide is what old American movies called a 'classy joint'. Stylistically out of step with the rest of the neighbourhood, the kitchen is often brilliantly inventive with dishes such as crab and salt cod cakes with roasted pepper and basil sauce.

Lodo Restaurant & Café ⑦

210 Hanover St

⊘ 617-720-0052

🔘 Subway to Haymarket

Open: Mon–Sat 1100–2230, Sun 1200–2230

Reservations recommended

All credit cards accepted

Italian

●●

Most diners get lost in the pastas and miss the point – Lodo is really a stylish seafood grill with broad windows that open on to the Hanover Street parade. The 'Extravaganza' feeds two people easily with mussels, scallops and half a lobster over *linguine*. Weekday luncheon specials are superb value.

Marcuccio's ⑧

125 Salem St

⊘ 617-723-1807

🔘 Subway to Haymarket

Open: daily 1700–2200

Reservations essential

All credit cards accepted

Italian

●●●

Chef Charles Draghi is a postmodernist cook steeped in the traditions of Abruzzi and Tuscany who can simultaneously wow the neighbourhood grandmothers and the out-of-town food critics. Make a night of it, ordering a course at a time – maybe starting with a chilled tomato soup with basil and rose essence and a plate of seared scallops with marjoram and walnut pesto. If you're perplexed by menu choices, choose the chef's signature sea bass.

Maurizio's ⑨

364 Hanover St

⊘ 617-367-1123

🔘 Subway to Haymarket

Open: lunch Wed–Sat 1200–1500; dinner Tue–Sat 1700–2200, Sun 1400–2200; closed Mon

Reservations recommended

All credit cards accepted

Italian

●●

Chef-owner Maurizio Lodo is a genius, and few restaurants are so consistently excellent at this price. Diners seated near the kitchen can watch Lodo work his seemingly effortless magic. Order any of the daily specials; the fish is particularly tasty.

Olives ⑩

10 City Sq, Charlestown

⊘ 617-242-1999

🔘 Bus #93 from Haymarket

Open: Mon–Sat 1730–2215, closed Sun

Reservations not allowed

 American Express

Italian–New American

●●●

Olives raises hearty Italian peasant food to an art. Portions are immense, and the quality is high, from perfect salads or an elegant asparagus tart with morel mushrooms to the roasted pork chop hanging off a mound of 'smashed' potatoes. Dine extra early to avoid a long wait.

Pomodoro ⑪

319 Hanover St

⊘ 617-367-4348

🔘 Subway to Haymarket

Open: daily 1100–2300

Reservations recommended

No credit cards accepted

Italian

●●

Pomodoro's eponymous tomato sauce is one of the North End's best, and this tiny trattoria elevates vegetables to star status. Even a non-vegetarian could be happy eating the cold grilled vegetable *antipasti*, great bread and warming soup.

▲ Old North End espresso machine

Artù 12

6 Prince St

Ⓢ Subway to Haymarket

Open: daily 1100–2300

VISA American Express

Roasted vegetables in all their individual glory define Artù, but honour must be paid to the extraordinary leg of lamb, available as thick pieces for dinner or thinly (but generously) sliced on sandwiches. Seating is tight, but the savoury cooking more than compensates.

Caffè Paradiso 13

255 Hanover St

Ⓢ Subway to Haymarket

Open: daily 0630–0200

VISA American Express

Modernistic Milano décor and a menu with sandwiches and salads set Paradiso apart from the longer-established neighbourhood *caffès*. The narrow space makes tables at the front look like a showcase, with rear tables as a retreat.

Café Pompeii 14

280 Hanover St

Ⓢ Subway to Haymarket

Open: daily 0900–0400

VISA

Homemade *gelati* and a no-smoking policy are the top reasons for visiting Pompeii, which also has a nice selection of grappas and sweet liqueurs, plus the longest hours in the neighbourhood.

Caffè Vittoria 15

296 Hanover St
🚇 Subway to Haymarket
Open: daily 0800–2400
No credit cards accepted

A plaque in the back of the café commemorates Enrico Caruso breaking into song here to prove his identity and cash a cheque. Two good reasons to patronise Vittoria are a jukebox with nearly all the songs by Frank Sinatra, Tony Bennett and Al Martino and separate smoking and non-smoking rooms.

Figs 16

67 Main St, Charlestown
🚌 Bus #93 from Haymarket
Open: Mon–Sat 1730–2200, Sun 1630–2100
💳 💳 American Express

Boston's grilled pizza craze began here; try one with caramelised figs, *prosciutto* and gorgonzola. The rich baked pastas are also stupendous, and the flourless chocolate cake is deep, dense and transporting. Almost every main course can comfortably feed two.

Ida's Restaurant 17

3 Mechanic St
🚇 Subway to Haymarket
Open: Tue–Sat 1700–2130, closed Sun–Mon
No credit cards accepted

Every dinner comes with spaghetti and salad, and almost every preparation can be assembled with chicken, veal or eggplant, making thoroughly old-fashioned Ida's a good bargain choice for vegetarians. The Bruno family is famously hospitable.

Il Panino Express 18

264–6 Hanover St
🚇 Subway to Haymarket
Open: daily 1100–2300
No credit cards accepted

Preparation of pizzas and pastas is down to a speedy science at this bustling corner that's a great spot for people watching. Good deals on excellent meals make Il Panino Express the North End's favourite Italian fast food stop.

Pat's Pushcart 19

61 Endicott St
🚇 Subway to Haymarket
Open: Tue–Sat 1700–2230, closed Sun–Mon
💳 💳

Pat's menu might be as old-fashioned as the red-and-white checked tablecloths and the Chianti in straw-covered bottles at this warm and welcoming restaurant. The food is tasty, the price is right and the house wine is more amiable than most. Pat's also makes single diners feel right at home.

Pizzeria Regina 20

11 Thacher St
🚇 Subway to Haymarket
Open: Mon–Sat 1100–2330, Sun 1200–2300
No credit cards accepted

This birthplace of a local pizza chain has the dark, atmospheric glaze of authenticity that its offspring lack. Somehow the thin-crust pies just taste better at this neighbourhood bar on a crazy angle in a jumble of tenement streets.

Umberto Rosticcría 21

289 Hanover St
🚇 Subway to Haymarket
Open: Mon–Sat 1100–1400, closed Sun
No credit cards accepted

Little more than an open hall with a counter at the rear, Umberto Rosticcría attracts North End *cognoscenti* for pizza, pasta, rice balls and other southern Italian lunch foods at rock bottom prices.

Warren Tavern 22

2 Pleasant St, Charlestown
🚌 Bus #93 from Haymarket
Open: Mon–Fri 1115–2230, Sat–Sun 1030–2230
💳 💳 American Express

The tavern is even older than nearby *Old Ironsides*, but the contemporary pub food more than passes muster. Lunch is a better deal than dinner.

NORTH END AND CHARLESTOWN
Shops, markets and picnic sites

Shops

A Bova & Sons Modern Bakery

134 Salem St

🚇 Subway to Haymarket

Open: 24 hours a day

VISA 💳

Baking fresh bread all day and serving pizza until after midnight, Bova is a requisite stop for a hot sandwich or a fistful of cookies after all the bars and cafés close.

Calore Fruit ㉔

99 Salem St

🚇 Subway to Haymarket

Open: daily 0700–1900

No credit cards accepted

This venerable fruit and fresh produce shop below street level consistently carries the finest quality fresh fruit from around the world.

Dairy Fresh Candies ㉖

57 Salem St

🚇 Subway to Haymarket

Open: Mon–Fri 0900–1800, Sat 0900–1900, Sun 1100–1800

VISA 💳 American Express

Local chocolates and a wide range of imported sweets make up the main stock of Dairy Fresh, but there's also a strong selection of spices, sauces, oils and vinegars.

Mike's Pastry

300 Hanover St

🚇 Subway to Haymarket

Open: Tue 0900–1800, Wed–Sat 0900–2200, Sun 0900–2000

No credit cards accepted

The neighbourhood's most popular pastry shop makes good *cannoli* and a huge selection of cakes, cookies and other sweets. A lucky few secure a café table to enjoy them with a steaming coffee or hot chocolate.

Monica's Salumeria ㉘

130 Salem St

🚇 Subway to Haymarket

Open: Mon–Sat 1100–2000, Sun 1200–2000

No credit cards accepted

Monica's sells the traditional Italian sausages and cheeses, but the *salumeria* specialises in prepared foods that range from cold salads to dishes for re-heating (eg, lasagne, eggplant *parmigiano*).

J Pace & Son ㉙

42 Cross St

🚇 Subway to Haymarket

Open: Mon–Sat 0700–1900, closed Sun

VISA 💳

From dried pastas and canned tomatoes to fresh cheeses and breads, Pace is a one-stop grocery for assembling a picnic or the ingredients to cook a Neapolitan feast.

Polcari's Coffee Shop ㉚

105 Salem St

🚇 Subway to Haymarket

Open: Mon–Sat 0830–1750, closed Sun

No credit cards accepted

In 1932 Polcari began providing Italian-roast coffee beans and was once New England's leading supplier of ground coffee for espresso. The family still sells coffee, along with a great selection of spices and coffeemakers.

Salumeria Italiana ㉛

151 Richmond St

🚇 Subway to Haymarket

Open: Mon–Sat 0800–1800, closed Sun

VISA 💳 American Express

Sausages, cheeses, olive oils and the requisite

canned goods for Italian cooking are the specialities of this great *salumeria* that has been a neighbourhood fixture as long as anyone can remember.

Trio's Ravioli Shoppe 32

222 Hanover St

🚇 Subway to Haymarket

Open: Mon–Sat 0900–1800, Sun 1000–1300

No credit cards accepted

The Trio family cranks out (and, in the case of tortellini, pinches) fresh pasta at this small store front. Goods are limited to the bare essentials: pasta and freshly prepared sauces.

V Cirace & Son, Inc 25

173 North St

🚇 Subway to Haymarket

Open: Mon–Thu 0900–2000, Fri–Sat 0900–2100, closed Sun

💳 American Express

Since 1906, Cirace has been the North End's select purveyor of Italian wines and liqueurs – both the great ones to lay down and the pleasant ones to drink immediately. Despite its refined look, Cirace stocks wines for every purse.

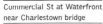

Picnic sites

Langone Park 33

Commercial St at Waterfront near Charlestown bridge

🚇 Subway to Haymarket

This grassy waterfront strip beneath the brow of Copp's Hill makes a fine spot to spread out a summer repast while looking across the mouth of the Charles River to Charlestown, where *Old Ironsides* is berthed.

Paul Revere Mall 34

Hanover St between Tileston and Charter Sts

🚇 Subway to Haymarket

Neighbourhood types call this mall 'the Prado', and you're likely to hear Italian being spoken by the cigar-smoking old men or the elderly ladies clad in black. An equestrian statue of revolutionary alarmist Paul Revere dominates the centre.

▲ Erminio Martignetti, owner of Salumeria Italiana

Boston wine and beer

Boozing in Boston

New England's climate is marginal, at best, for the delicate *vinifera* grapes used to make the world's best table wines. But eastern Massachusetts does boast one winery that has confounded expectation. Blessed with a gentle microclimate on Buzzards Bay, the winemakers at **Westport Rivers Winery**, about an hour's drive south of Boston, produce primarily cool-climate white wines from Riesling and Chardonnay grapes. Their sparkling wines, made in the labour-intensive *méthode champenoise*, are consistent international award winners and can be found on the lists of about 50 of Boston's best restaurants.

Beer-drinkers will find even more variety in their favoured beverage thanks to the revival of the Boston brewing industry in the 1980s. Two superb 'craft' breweries produce small batches of beer in bottles and kegs for local bars and restaurants and for sale in stores.

The **Boston Beer Company** (*30 Germania St, Jamaica Plain; Ø 617-368-5080*) is one of the best known 'microbreweries' in the USA, producing its flagship **Samuel Adams Lager** and a seasonally varying mix of other lagers, ales, porters and bocks. **Tremont Brewery** (*50 Terminal St, Charlestown; Ø 617-242-6464*) is primarily a producer of ales, and many Boston drinkers swear by the draught version of the flagship **Tremont Ale**. Both breweries offer tours and tastings.

The local 'brewpubs' make their own ales on the premises and generally affect a heartier, more European style than is common with most North American brewers. Boston beer tends to be brewed with stronger-tasting and darker malt and more bitter hops than, say, the beers of the Pacific Northwest, which generally aim for a light malt and aromatic hops.

Located a few blocks from Faneuil Hall Marketplace toward the Fleet Center, **Commonwealth Fish & Beer** (*138 Portland St; Ø 617-523-8383; ❻❻*) was the city's first brewpub and its immense copper kettles figure prominently in the décor. The best fish main courses are grilled, such as the pepper-crusted tuna served with mango salsa. For more traditional beer food, order the slow-roasted baby back ribs.

The **Back Bay Brewing Co.** (*755 Boylston St; Ø 617-424-8300; ❻❻*) serves as a prime spot for socialising on upper Boylston

Street. Brewer Tod Mott crafts ales with depth and flair, and it's worth trying the 'beer sampler' of all six available brews in five-ounce glasses. Beef is the best bet on the menu – either the garlic-crusted sirloin steak or the mammoth 'Back Bay burger'.

The **Boston Beer Works** (*61 Brookline Ave; ⌀ 617-536-2337; ❸❸*) sits at the edge of the Boston University campus across the street from the baseball Mecca of Fenway Park. Location alone ensures a steady supply of patrons. The ales are serviceable if often *very* cold, and the menu features pastas, salads and grilled meats. The mixed grill plate will easily feed four very hungry carnivores.

The **Brew Moon Restaurant** (*115 Tremont St, ⌀ 617-523-6467, ❸❸; also 50 Church St, Cambridge, ⌀ 617-499-2739, ❸❸*) is easily the quirkiest of Boston brewpubs, with flashy décor and an ambitious menu that incorporates beer into almost everything, including the desserts. The Brew Moon sometimes makes 'cute' beers, such as raspberry white beer. On the other hand, its porter is satisfyingly traditional.

The progenitor of a regional brewpub chain, **John Harvard's Brew House** (*33 Dunster St, Cambridge; ⌀ 617-868-3585; ❸❸*) stands only steps from the site of Massachusetts' first brewery, licensed in 1636. The crisp, sharply hopped **India Pale Ale**

▲ Outdoor tables at the Back Bay Brewing Co.

attests to the brewmaster's skills and it is nicely complemented by the food, which includes an ale-and-mustard roast chicken. Free live music begins at 2200 on Sunday and Monday.

It's worth going out of your way to visit the **North East Brewing Company** (*1314 Commonwealth Ave, Allston; ⌀ 617-566-6699; ⊚ subway: Green Line 'B', Griggs St/Long Ave stop; ❸❸*), where 8 to 12 freshly brewed beers are on tap daily. Head brewer Dann Paquette regularly gets placed in the top three at major national competitions and chef Thomas Shea makes liberal use of beers in the cuisine, flavouring beef gravy with stout, for example. Live music (no cover) is also free-flowing from Wednesday to Saturday nights.

> **Boston beer tends to be brewed with stronger-tasting and darker malt and more bitter hops than other beers of the Pacific Northwest.**

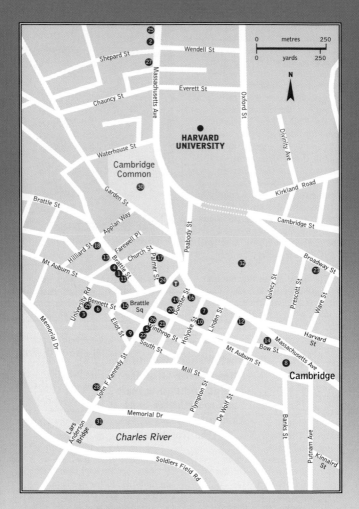

Harvard Square

Youthful and bustling Harvard Square has a healthy concentration of inexpensive, ethnic restaurants popular with the student trade, as well as several of Boston's more sophisticated dining destinations. Street performers and the milling human parade enliven the pavement-dining scene.

Casablanca ❶

40 Brattle St, Cambridge

✆ 617-876-0999

🔘 Subway to Harvard Sq

Open: lunch 1130–1430;
dinner Sun–Thu 1730–2200,
Fri–Sat 1730–2300

Reservations recommended

All credit cards accepted

Mediterranean

❷❸

As the name implies,
Casablanca approaches
Mediterranean cuisine
from North Africa.
Don't miss the bright
Arabian treatments of
otherwise pungent blue-
fish, the killer *cassoulet*
or the spicy meatballs of
lamb and bulgar wheat.
The great bar in rear is
a time-honoured literary
watering hole.

Chez Henri ❷

1 Shepard St, Cambridge

✆ 617-354-8980

🔘 Subway to Harvard Sq

Open: Mon–Thu 1800–2200,
Fri–Sat 1730–2300, Sun
1730–2100

Reservations not allowed

All credit cards accepted

French-Caribbean

❷❸

On the outer orbit of the
square, Chez Henri is
worth the walk for
French bistro fare with
a Cuban accent in a
room with Parisian
panache. The convivial,
if cramped, bar serves
some of the dining
room items (such as the
legendary duck tamales)
and Boston's favourite
cubano sandwiches.

▲ Chef Ana Sortun of Casablanca

Giannino

20 University Road (Charles Hotel Courtyard), Cambridge

✆ 617-576-0605

Ⓜ Subway to Harvard Sq

Open: daily 1100–2300

Reservations recommended

All credit cards accepted

Italian

💲💲

Elegant Northern Italian fare emphasising roasted meats and fish sets Giannino apart from the plethora of red-sauce Italian eateries. For light eaters, most meat or fish main courses are available in half portions. The superb wine list has an unusually good range of Tuscan and Piedmont labels, and the limited outdoor seating has a long waiting list in the summer.

Harvest ④

44 Brattle St, Cambridge

✆ 617-868-2255

Ⓜ Subway to Harvard Sq

Open: lunch Mon–Sat 1200–1430; tea Mon–Sun 1430–1700; dinner Mon–Thu 1730–2230, Fri–Sat 1700–2300, Sun 1730–2200

Reservations essential

All credit cards accepted

New American

💲💲💲

Top young chefs have cut their teeth at Harvest for more than two decades. The current incarnation emphasises up-market, French-influenced treatments of local fish and gourmet produce, but

carnivores can also relish some of Boston's biggest, juiciest steaks.

Iruña ⑤

56 John F Kennedy St, Cambridge

✆ 617-868-5633

Ⓜ Subway to Harvard Sq

Open: lunch Mon–Fri 1200–1400; dinner Mon–Thu 1800–2100, Fri 1800–2200, Sat 1330–2200; closed Sun

Reservations unnecessary

🔲 💳 American Express Discover

Spanish

💲💲

A long-time Harvard favourite, especially among poets on a spree, Iruña's best dishes are generally Basque. The garlicky squid, for example, are superb. Watch carefully for the sign, as the restaurant sits well off the street.

Rialto ⑥

Charles Hotel, 1 Bennett St, Cambridge

✆ 617-661-5050

Ⓜ Subway to Harvard Sq

Open: Sun–Thu 1730–2145, Fri–Sat 1730–2245

Reservations essential

All credit cards accepted

Mediterranean

💲💲💲

Any Boston visitor who is serious about food should reserve a table at Rialto. The décor is smart and sophisticated and the service friendly and helpful. But what sets Rialto apart is chef Jody Adams' luscious

approach to the classic cuisines of the sun, where rosemary is magic and basil a herb to conjure with.

Sandrine's Bistro ⑦

8 Holyoke St, Cambridge

✆ 617-497-5300

Ⓜ Subway to Harvard Sq

Open: lunch Tue–Sat 1130–1430; dinner Sun–Wed 1730–2130, Thu–Sat 1730–2230

Reservations recommended

🔲 💳 American Express

French

💲💲

Of Boston's many French restaurants, only Sandrine's is Alsatian, specialising in hearty dishes of the Strasbourg region, including a homemade *choucroute garni* with enough meat to feed a family. Sandrine's signature dish is *flammekueche* – a flame-baked flatbread with toppings that's also available as a snack at the bar.

Siam Garden ⑧

45 Mt. Auburn St, Cambridge

✆ 617-354-1718

Ⓜ Subway to Harvard Sq

Open: daily 1200–2200

Reservations unnecessary

All credit cards accepted

Thai-Vegetarian

💲

Although Boston has slicker and more modern Thai restaurants, Siam Garden pioneered the subtle cuisine with its many curries and holy basil. Delightfully old-fashioned with straight-back chairs and cloth table coverings, Siam Garden remains extremely popular as a student date destination.

Tanjore ⑨

18 Eliot St, Cambridge	
⌀ 617-868-1900	
⊙ Subway to Harvard Sq	
Open: lunch 1130–1530; dinner 1630–2300	
Reservations recommended	
💳 💳 Discover	
Indian	
⑤	

At dinner, Tanjore offers an unusually sophisticated presenta-tion of specialities from the different regions of India, with an emphasis on the roasted meats of the northwest. The midday buffet luncheon maintains the high standard at low prices.

Up Stairs at the Pudding ⑩

10 Holyoke St, Cambridge	
⌀ 617-864-1933	
⊙ Subway to Harvard Sq	
Open: lunch Mon–Fri 1130–1430, Sat 1130–1400; Sun brunch 1100–1400; dinner Mon–Sat 1730–2200, Sun 1730–2130	
Reservations essential	
All credit cards accepted	
Italian-French	
⑤⑤⑤	

Up Stairs at the Pudding (located over the Hasty Pudding Theatre) is the likely room to spot Harvard University's old guard as they toast Epicurus with full-bodied burgundies amid posters of Pudding productions. At its best, Up Stairs is simultane-ously decadent and subtle, with dishes such as the saffron cream lobster soup. In warm weather, the rooftop garden is a splendid spot for a sumptuous lunch. The à la carte Sunday brunch is a local favourite throughout the year.

▲ Enjoying an Alsatian meal at Sandrine's Bistro

HARVARD SQUARE
Bars, cafés and pubs

Algiers Coffee House ⑪

40 Brattle St, Cambridge

◉ Subway to Harvard Sq

Open: daily 0800–2400

All credit cards accepted

Probably the only Cambridge café where 'health food' and second-hand smoke mingle, Algiers has a terrific, inexpensive midday buffet of salads, chickpeas, feta cheese and breads. The air is blue in the upstairs smoking section.

Bartley's Burger Cottage ⑫

1246 Massachusetts Ave, Cambridge

◉ Subway to Harvard Sq

Open: Mon–Wed, Sat 1100–2100, Thu–Fri 1100–2200, closed Sun

Grab a fistful of ground beef in this Harvard institution where burgers and sandwiches with insufferably cute names offer inexpensive sustenance.

Café Pamplona ⑭

8 Bow St, Cambridge

◉ Subway to Harvard Sq

Open: Mon–Sat 1100–0100, Sun 1400–0100

Shades of young Hemingway – the coffee is strong and small, the sandwiches austere but tasty. On a bone-chilling night, nothing

▲ Pavement dining at Bartley's Burger Cottage

is quite as warming as Pamplona's *sopa de ajo* (garlic soup).

Caffè Paradiso ⑮

1 Elliot Sq, Cambridge

🚇 Subway to Harvard Sq

Open: Sun–Thu 0700–2300, Fri–Sat 0700–2430

American Express Discover

Definitely the prime spot to be seen for the gold-chain-and-chest-hair crowd, Paradiso has outdoor tables and intense coffee to provide a lift while you watch the world go past.

Campo de' Fiori ⑯

1352 Massachusetts Ave (Holyoke Center), Cambridge

🚇 Subway to Harvard Sq

Open: Mon–Fri 0800–2000, Sat 1100–1800, closed Sun

American Express

The speciality in this tiny Italian outlet inside a Harvard shopping-cum-office centre is *pane romano*, long rectangles of flatbread topped with everything from Nutella (for breakfast) to sausage and cheese for lunchtime snacks.

Club Passim ⑰

47 Palmer St, Cambridge

🚇 Subway to Harvard Sq

Open: daily 1100–2300

Chickpeas, yoghurt, grape leaves and other Asia Minor standards at lunch and dinner aren't as big a draw as the evening folksingers in the club known for

launching the careers of many singer-song-writers.

Hi Rise Bread Company ⑱

56 Brattle St (Blacksmith House), Cambridge

🚇 Subway to Harvard Sq

Open: Mon–Fri 0830–1700, Sat 0900–1700, closed Sun

The bakery's great breads make super sandwiches. Vegetarians can enjoy several sandwich and salad choices. Head upstairs for self-service seating at long wooden tables.

L A Burdick ⑬

52D Brattle St, Cambridge

🚇 Subway to Harvard Sq

Open: Tue–Sat 0800–2300, Sun–Mon 0900–2100

American Express Discover

Elegant dipped chocolates abound and a small pastry selection is available, but knowledgeable customers come to drink the hot chocolate – available in milk, dark or white chocolate.

Lee's Beehive ⑲

24 Dunster St, Cambridge

🚇 Subway to Harvard Sq

Open: Mon–Fri 0700–2100, Sat 0800–2100, Sun 0900–2100

The Beehive is the last of a dying breed of all-American grill and sandwich shops, sure to become a retro fad when the last real one passes. Hearty breakfast specials and sandwiches

are the particular highlights.

Ma Soba ⑳

30 Dunster St, Cambridge

🚇 Subway to Harvard Sq

Open: daily 1100–2400

Noodles, noodles, noodles everywhere! Ma Soba's eclectic selections of Chinese, Japanese, Malaysian and southeast Asian noodle dishes are served cafeteria-style, making Ma Soba a quick as well as cheap stop.

Pinocchio's ㉑

74 Winthrop St, Cambridge

🚇 Subway to Harvard Sq

Open: Mon–Sat 1100–0200, Sun 1100–2400

Whether for thick crust or thin, this hole-in-the-wall pizza joint is a Cambridge institution. Don't look for designer pizzas, just the classics. Seating is limited.

Shay's Pub & Wine Bar ㉒

58 John F Kennedy St, Cambridge

🚇 Subway to Harvard Sq

Open: Mon–Sat 1100–0100, Sun 1200–0100

All credit cards accepted

Shay's seems to be the hangout for well-tanned, sports-minded Harvard types. The beer is cold, the burgers are hot, and the sunken outdoor tables are highly coveted in warm weather.

HARVARD SQUARE
Shops, markets and picnic sites

Shops

Broadway Marketplace

486 Broadway, Cambridge

🚇 Subway to Harvard Sq

Open: Mon–Sat 0700–2100, Sun 0900–1900

All credit cards accepted

Only a block from the Harvard Art Museums, Broadway has outstanding fruit and vegetable selections, almost every cooking staple, and good deli and bakery cases. Ready-to-cook meals are handy if you have self-catering lodgings.

Cardullo's Gourmet Shoppe ㉔

6 Brattle St, Cambridge

🚇 Subway to Harvard Sq

Open: Mon–Fri 0800–2000, Sat 0900–2100, Sun 1100–1900

💳 💳 American Express Discover

Looking for tinned *pâté de foie gras*? Belgian chocolates? German and Swiss brands of herbal tea? Cardullo's is the likeliest spot to find them (at a price). It's also a good choice for midday deli meat and cheese sandwiches.

Evergood Fine Foods ㉕

1674 Massachusetts Ave, Cambridge

🚇 Subway to Harvard Sq

Open: Mon–Sat 0800–1900, Sun 1000–1800

💳 💳

A cut above the usual convenience market, Evergood has a small selection of organic fruits and vegetables as well as free-range chicken. The chewy breads from Iggy's are among the best around.

Look for bread pudding and grapenut pudding in the rear cooler.

Harvard Provision Company 26

94 Mt Auburn St, Cambridge

🔵 Subway to Harvard Sq

Open: Mon–Wed 0900–2155, Thu–Fri 0900–2255, Sat 1000–2255, closed Sun

💳 American Express

Easy to miss from the street, Harvard Provision has the best selection of wines at the keenest prices in or near the square. Their 'specials' bins tend to feature high-value obscure wines at low cost. Remember: it's for behind closed doors, not your picnic. It's illegal to drink wine outdoors in Massachusetts.

Montrose 27

1646 Massachusetts Ave, Cambridge

🔵 Subway to Harvard Sq

Open: daily 0700–2300

💳

The Cuban owners of this store carry Caribbean produce and staples as well as standard American fare. The deli also makes the most authentic *cubano* sandwich in the city, importing the roasted pork loin from New York.

Markets

Harvard Square Farmers' Market 29

Charles Sq (Charles Hotel entrance plaza), Cambridge

🔵 Subway to Harvard Sq

Open: Sun 1000–1300

Area farmers bring freshly picked vegetables, fruits and flowers to this small public market every Sun morning from May to October. Look for strawberries and raspberries in June and July, peaches in August and apples thereafter.

Picnic sites

Cambridge Common 30

Bounded by Massachusetts Ave, Garden St and Waterbridge St

🔵 Subway to Harvard Sq

The triangular green north from Harvard Square is dotted with playing fields and is criss-crossed with pavements, but you can still spread out an al fresco picnic on the green lawn beneath a scion of the elm tree where George Washington assumed command of the Continental Army.

Charles Riverbank 31

Between Memorial Drive and Charles River, from Lars Anderson Bridge (JFK St) south to Western Ave bridge

🔵 Subway to Harvard Sq

The greensward of the Charles riverbank serves as Harvard's tanning beach on sunny summer days, but it's also a lively place to plop down for a takeaway meal. Stake out a patch of grass between the paved inline and bicycle path and the worn-dirt running track to watch the rowers glide by.

Harvard Yard 32

Bounded by Massachusetts Ave, Broadway, and Peabody and Quincy Sts

🔵 Subway to Harvard Sq

Green grass unrolls like a carpet beneath the leafy canopy of ancient trees in the oh-so-collegiate preserve of Harvard Yard. The Yard is theoretically off-limits to loitering non-students. For camouflage, stick your nose in a volume of Hume and watch out for flying frisbees.

John F Kennedy Park 28

Corner of JFK St and Memorial Drive

This broad grassy triangle was once slated over for the JFK Library and Museum, but evolved into one of the least used but most delightful parks in Cambridge when the Library was built on Columbia Point instead. Lounge on the lawn beneath stately maples or take a stone bench seat at the fountain, where you can evaluate yourself by JFK's measures of history: 'We were truly men of courage ... of judgement ... of integrity ... of dedication?' Did you remember the mustard?

Cool sweets

I scream, you scream, we all scream for ice cream
– American children's chant

According to national studies, Bostonians eat more ice cream per capita than anyone else in the world and about 50 per cent more than the average American. Part of the credit (or blame) lies with entrepreneur Steve Herrell. In the early 1970s he opened a tiny shop in Somerville where he introduced what has become known as **'super-premium' ice cream** – a version of the dairy concoction made with an unusually high butterfat content. Much of the original appeal was its 'homemade' moniker, denoting small batches of carefully blended ingredients.

Steve's Ice Cream was an instant success, although only one outlet remains (*Faneuil Hall Marketplace; ✆ 617-367-0569;*

✆). Steve's spawned a multitude of imitators, feeding into a nationwide craze for corporate super-premium ice creams. The most prominent survivor of the ice cream wars is Vermont-based **Ben & Jerry's** (*174 Newbury St; ✆ 617-536-5456; ✆*). Ben & Jerry's products often have whimsical names such as 'Chunky Monkey' (banana and chocolate).

Herrell went on to establish a second chain with several local outposts, including **Herrell's Ice Cream** (*15 Dunster St, Cambridge; ✆ 617-497-2179; ✆*) and **Herrell's Ice Cream & Espresso Bar** (*224 Newbury St; ✆ 617-236-0857; ✆*). In addition to a bewildering range of flavours that change every day, these shops also offer 'smoosh-ins' – nuts, broken cookies and pieces of candy that are mashed into the ice cream just before serving.

To counter the essentially juvenile character of such sweets, **Toscanini's** (*889 Main St, Cambridge, ✆ 617-491-5877; and 1310 Massachusetts Ave, Cambridge, ✆ 617-354-9350; ✆*) launched super-premium ice creams with refined flavours designed to appeal to adults. Among the subtle varieties usually on the menu are saffron, green tea, and burnt caramel. Chocoholics are also well-served with standard choices of white chocolate, Belgian chocolate and mocha Toscanini's offers only one topping – hot fudge sauce – but it is arguably the finest in Boston.

New Englanders in general and Bostonians in particular are very fussy about their ice cream fountain drinks. In Boston a 'milkshake' includes milk and flavoured syrup. To get the drink blended with ice cream requires asking for a 'frappe' (pronounced 'frap'). The old-fashioned ice cream soda has become very difficult to find. The best in the city are made at **Christina's Homemade Ice Cream** (*1255 Cambridge St, Inman Sq, Cambridge; ✆ 617-492-7021; ❸*). This concoction consists of flavoured syrup and cream fizzed with seltzer water and topped with a scoop of ice cream.

Even before the advent of Steve Herrell, Bostonians were scooping up hot fudge sundaes (ice cream topped with hot fudge sauce) or simply licking scoops dipped in 'chocolate jimmies' (chocolate shot) and planted in simple sugar wafer cones at **Brigham's** (*189 Cambridge St, ✆ 617-523-9822; also 50 Congress St, ✆ 617-523-9372; and 109 High St, ✆ 617-482-3524; ❸*). This venerable chain, based in nearby Arlington, also serves sandwiches, breakfast and light grill food.

The deplorable health- and weight-consciousness that periodically sweeps the USA like a plague has not entirely spared the Boston emporia of super-premium ice creams. But they

▲ Everyone loves ice cream in Boston

have adapted to the times by augmenting their offerings with lower-fat frozen yoghurts and even water ices.

European-style ice creams and frozen desserts still have their Boston adherents. The more-or-less French **Café de Paris** (*19 Arlington St; ✆ 617-247-7121; ❸*) emulates the cafés of the City of Light by offering mounded concoctions of ice cream, sauces, chopped nuts and fluffy chantilly that go by names that suggest exotic locales and high peaks: Kashmir, Zebra, Kilimanjaro. The pleasures of traditional Italian *gelati* are not lost on Bostonians either. *Caffès* of the North End have cases with at least a dozen flavours, and even Boston Brahmins indulge in the Beacon Hill *gelati* of the venerable **Caffè Bella Vita** (*30 Charles St; ✆ 617-720-4504; ❸*). The best bet for newcomers is the mixture of vanilla with flakes of bitter chocolate, stracciatella.

> **Bostonians eat more ice cream per capita than anyone else in the world and about 50 per cent more than the average American.**

Food etiquette and culture

FOOD ETIQUETTE AND CULTURE

Dining in Boston is more than just a meal – it's evolved into one of the city's most widespread forms of evening entertainment. In general terms, you'll want to head to the North End for Italian and Italian-inspired food, to the Waterfront for seafood, to Chinatown for all forms of Asian cuisine, and to Back Bay, the South End and Harvard Square for cutting-edge cuisine from some of the city's most prominent chefs. Lunch stops that serve good food quickly are most abundant in Downtown and the Financial District.

MEAL TIMES

Dining hours in Boston are comparable to the rest of the USA. Breakfast is served at most restaurants from 0800 until 1000, although certain cafés near hospitals and other all-night establishments sometimes begin breakfast as early as 0400 and continue serving until 1200. Boston keeps rather narrow lunch hours, with dining rooms opening around 1130 and beginning to close at around 1330. After 1400 it can be difficult to find a dining room lunch, although cafés and coffee shops usually continue serving until 1600. Dinner hours are somewhat more flexible. Some extremely popular restaurants open as early as 1730, and almost all begin serving by 1800. During the week, few will seat diners after 2100 or after 2200 on Friday and Saturday. The most popular times to dine are between 1900 and 2100, although early tables are at a premium in restaurants near the Theatre District.

SECURING A TABLE

With some notable exceptions (many North End establishments, Olives in Charlestown, Chez Henri in Harvard Sq), most restaurants accept advance bookings. At those that don't make bookings, diners who arrive when the doors open have the best chance of immediate seating. Many restaurants that otherwise follow a first-come, first-served policy will accept bookings for parties of six or more diners, especially on weeknights.

Boston's most prestigious restaurants are often booked weeks ahead, but the city's restaurateurs are surprisingly congenial, so if your first choice is fully booked, ask for another recommendation or sweat it out on the waiting list. Don't hesitate to call at the last minute, as cancellations are common. Once a booking is made, be sure to appear on time or not more than 15 minutes late (blame it on the traffic). If you are running late, call ahead and the restaurant might be able to adjust your reservation.

SMOKING

Restrictions on smoking in Boston and Cambridge are among the most stringent in the USA, and smoking is generally banned in dining rooms but permitted in most bars. Cambridge does not permit minors to be seated in a smoking area. Smoking is generally permitted at outdoor tables, contributing to the popularity of al fresco dining.

MOBILE PHONES

Check with individual restaurants for policies on the use of cellular telephones and personal beepers. Some restaurants ban their use or ask that you leave the devices with the *maître d'* to allow others to dine in uninterrupted peace. Even in restaurants without such policies, the use of a telephone at the table is considered a breach of good etiquette. Like smoking, phones and beepers are acceptable at outdoor tables and in bars, although their use will be frowned upon by other diners.

PORTIONS

Fine dining restaurants in Boston have a tendency to serve super-size portions. If you have a fridge available, do not hesitate to ask for 'a doggy bag', the euphemism for 'tomorrow's lunch'. Many restaurants expect you to ask, and waiters might fear that you didn't enjoy the meal if you decline to take home the half you were unable to finish.

Given the large portions, it is an increasingly common practice for two diners to split an appetiser and each order a main course – or even vice versa. Some restaurants state a minimum charge per person on the menu and might levy a 'plating charge' for splitting a dish between two people. Do not be hesitant to order less rather than more, or to make a meal of two appetisers.

TIPPING

Tipping has escalated from the old days when 10 per cent would ensure that the waiter or waitress remembered your name. At a fine-dining establishment, a 15 per cent tip is considered the absolute minimum for good service, to be augmented if you're feeling particularly expansive, if you have received a high level of service or have made a number of special requests. Moreover, it is standard practice to tip 10 per cent to the servers at a buffet meal. Bartenders expect 50 cents to $1 per drink.

Menu decoder

Despite its Puritan origins and strong links to the UK, Boston is a cosmopolitan city of striking ethnic diversity. This multiculturalism is reflected in the city's restaurants, where it is possible to dine on everything from Thai green curry to Yucatecan baked fish or Alsatian *choucroute* to steamed dumplings made in the style of Guangdong province. Yet apart from the distinctly ethnic restaurants, often operated by new immigrants, Boston has evolved a complex cuisine of its own, born of centuries of cultural overlays and the bounty of nearby fields and waters.

TRADITIONAL NEW ENGLAND COOKERY

Traditional Bostonian cuisine is a fusion of the Anglo-Saxon cookery brought by the first European settlers with the Native American foods they encountered once they arrived. Indigenous North American food plants – maize, beans, maple, and hard

squashes such as pumpkin – remain key ingredients in Boston cooking, whether in old-fashioned dishes such as *succotash* (beans and maize), baked beans or roasted Hubbard squash, or in such contemporary treatments as maple polenta cakes. The British influences are equally strong, with dishes such as pot roast (braised beef roast), boiled dinner (pot roast cooked with root vegetables), and fruit pies. Although not confined to Boston, Parker House rolls (a fluffy yeasted dinner roll), toll-house cookies (chocolate chips in a chewy butter-and-brown-sugar cookie) and Boston cream pie (layers of yellow cake with a custard filling and chocolate ganache topping) were invented in or near Boston.

Until about 1970 this British-influenced style of New England 'home cooking' utterly dominated the Boston dining scene, and it persists in many casual neighbourhood restaurants, luncheonettes and cafés that advertise 'home-style' food. Its more elegant forms also still reign in a handful of tradition-bound fine-dining establishments, where beef Wellington (a pastry-encased roast) is considered the height of culinary daring.

NEW AMERICAN COOKING

Thanks to several innovative chefs and cookbook authors, Boston was in the vanguard of the revolution in cooking and dining that began to sweep the USA in the 1970s. As American minds opened and tastes broadened, more adventurous cooking became the norm. In Boston a spate of new restaurants began serving French provincial cooking, northern Italian food and other cuisines of the Mediterranean basin. In many neighbourhoods 'restaurants' disappeared in favour of 'bistros' and 'trattorias', and this style of casual country cooking inspired by Mediterranean traditions remains the single most popular style in Boston. Diners will be hard-pressed to find a meal without garlic and the classic southern European culinary herbs.

But even beyond the adoption of Continental cuisines, Boston chefs began to turn their attention to fresh ingredients available close at hand. New American cooking, as it came to be known, is a combination of the oldest cooking in the world – fresh-market cuisine – with the American penchant for fusing a world of influences into a single hybrid identity.

At their best, the chefs who favour this style look at cooking less as a task than as an art. They are apt to synthesise dishes by adapting ingredients, techniques and flavourings from a broad palette of choices. In the New American style, a traditional Boston Independence Day dinner of baked salmon with fresh green peas and steamed new potatoes might be rendered as an appetiser dish of chef-cured gravlax (a salt and sugar cure for fresh fish) with quickly steamed pea tendrils and a dab of practically

luminescent green *wasabi* (Japanese horseradish) – all served with chickpea-meal black-pepper crackers.

One salutary effect that New American cooking has had on Boston dining is the advent of the self-explanatory menu. Once upon a time a diner had to know that 'Florentine' meant that a dish contained spinach. But since New American dishes, almost by definition, depart from the tried and tested, chefs often feel compelled to explain themselves on their menus. At its most extreme, this tendency can become comical, as it could take longer to read the menu description than to eat the dish. But it does help the diner make decisions by mentally weighing the flavour combinations.

GREAT NEW ENGLAND FOODS

Diners might also observe that some Boston chefs use their menus to credit sources for key ingredients. A specific grower of *mâché* or baby lettuces might be listed for certain salad fixings, while individual fishmongers might be identified as providing the mussels or clams for a particular dish. Once moribund, New England agriculture has had a revival in order to cater to the demanding needs of chefs throughout the region, but especially in Boston.

Most chefs introduce a new menu at least every season, and some every few weeks. A chef who suddenly discovers he can get a crate of freshly picked fiddlehead ferns (a delectable, nutty green available for about two weeks each spring) might scratch half the standard menu to build dishes around the fiddleheads while they last.

In similar fashion, dishes (both sweet and savoury) that depend on fresh fruit will change with the sequence of the local harvest of strawberries in June, raspberries and cultivated blueberries in July, tiny wild blueberries in early August, followed by peaches, apples and pears and the final autumn batch of jewel-like red raspberries. New England also grows about 40 per cent of the world's cranberries, and they tend to brighten Boston menus from the late autumn into the dead of winter.

Even the entire cuisine might seem to shift at some restaurants – especially in July when local tomatoes, peppers and corn (maize) come into season and menus begin to look downright Mediterranean as many cooks attempt to tame the bounty by cooking it down into sauces.

This seasonality affects more than produce. The New England cheese industry has undergone a heartening renaissance, and Boston chefs are well attuned to the nuances of cheeses made locally in small batches. Vermont has been known for its aged cheddars for more than a century, but small dairies specialising in blue cheese, fresh goats' cheese and sheeps' milk cheeses have sprung up around the region. Many of these cheese-makers simply refrain from producing cheeses when their milking animals are reduced to eating winter-feed. As a result, fresh cheeses (or dishes made with them) abound on menus in the summer and early autumn, aged cheeses during the winter and spring.

SEAFOOD

The oceans off Boston supplied the colonists with a bounty of fish and shellfish similar to, if not always identical to, those found in the British Isles. Indeed, many fish species long ago fished to extinction in northern Europe flourish in the cold New England coastal waters and make regular appearances on Boston menus.

Boston chefs tend to feature the mild, white-fleshed, flaky sea bass or striped bass, codfish,

haddock, halibut and flounder in roasted or fried dishes. So-called 'scrod' (also spelled 'schrod') is usually a small cod or haddock. For grilled main courses, chefs tend to feature rich-flavoured, dark-fleshed blue fin tuna, *mahi-mahi* (Americans confuse the traditional appellation 'dolphin' with beloved porpoises), and swordfish. Many chefs substitute *mako* shark for swordfish to assist with the revival of dwindling swordfish stocks. Oily and strong-flavoured bluefish is also sometimes offered in late summer, usually roasted with mustard or sometimes smoked.

Limitations on traditional fisheries have introduced under-utilised species to Boston plates, notably monkfish, skate, octopus and squid. Fish farming is also on the rise, with the happy result that fresh Atlantic salmon, sea bass, *tilapia* (a South American pan fish) and mussels are always available.

Local shellfish are plentiful and superb. Boston claims clam chowder (with milk, no tomato) as its own. Clams are classified as 'chowder clams' (the smallest, tenderest ones), 'steamers' (small clams both steamed and fried), and 'quahogs' (a Wampanoag Indian name for larger clams often roasted and stuffed). Scallops come as sea scallops (large chunks) or the tinier, more tender 'bay scallops', which are also sometimes steamed like clams. Steamed bowls of the common black mussel, both farmed and wild, have become a staple on many menus.

Although not the most plenti-ful bivalve, nor the most common on Boston menus, local oysters rank among some of the finest in the world. They are at their best in the spring, when the water is still very cold. The best of them are American bluepoint oysters from Cape Cod and Nantucket Island. Connoisseurs claim that Wellfleet oysters, in particular, are the best of the best.

Except in Chinatown, whole crabs show up infrequently on Boston menus, as the flesh from small New England blue and rock crabs usually ends up in crab cakes and as crabmeat salad. One exception is during July, when crabs shed their shells and whole fried 'soft shell crab' is ubiquitous.

The king of the sea in Boston remains the Maine lobster (*homarus americanus*), the brawnier and more tasty relative of the northern European lobster, *homarus vulgaris*. 'Soft-shell' lobster dominates the market from July to September, when the crustaceans shed their shells and grow oversized new ones. Traditionally, lobster is steamed whole and served with melted butter, with a hammer to crush the shells and small picks to remove the meat. The only *de rigueur* accompaniments are a buttered ear of steamed corn and a slice of blueberry pie.

Recipes

Boston baked beans
(recipe courtesy of Durgin Park)

Baked beans have been a standard in Boston cuisine since the earliest days of the Massachusetts Bay Colony. The Boston preference for molasses with beans dates from the city's extensive trade with the Caribbean, when Boston ships brought home molasses to distil into rum. Traditionally, Boston homemakers would take their bean pots to the bakery for slow cooking overnight in a cooling oven. Baked beans, steamed brown bread and hot dogs are a Saturday night tradition.

Serves 10

INGREDIENTS

2-quart bean pot	
2/3 cups molasses	
2 pounds beans – California pea beans preferred or York State beans	
2 teaspoons dry mustard	
4 teaspoons salt	
1 pound salt pork	
½ teaspoon pepper	
8 tablespoons sugar	
1 medium-sized onion	

Soak the beans overnight. In the morning parboil them for ten minutes with a teaspoon of baking soda. Then run cold water through the beans in a colander or strainer. Dice the salt pork rind into inch squares, then cut them in half. Put

▲ Boston baked beans with 'franks' and cornbread

half on the bottom of the bean pot with the whole onion. Put the beans in the pot. Put the rest of the pork on top. Mix the other ingredients with hot water and then pour it over beans. Put the pot into a 300°F oven for six hours.

Clam chowder
(recipe courtesy of Turner Fisheries)

Clam chowder as it's prepared in Boston and throughout northern New England invariably includes milk or cream, whereas 'Manhattan clam chowder' employs tomato juice as part of the liquid. The Turner Fisheries version has won so many chowder contests that it has been officially 'retired'. Chowder is more a stew than a soup and is traditionally served with baking powder biscuits or 'oyster crackers' (small, round soda crackers).

Serves 10

INGREDIENTS

10 cherrystone clams	
6 quahog clams	
1 medium onion, chopped	
1 stick of celery, diced	
1 large potato, diced	
40oz clam juice	
1 pint heavy cream	
1 cup water	
4oz clarified butter	
4oz flour	
1 bay leaf	
½ teaspoon white pepper	
1 clove garlic, minced	
½ teaspoon thyme	

▲ Turner Fisheries' clam chowder

Wash the clams thoroughly. Place the quahog clams in pot with half a cup of water. Cover tightly and steam until the clams open. Repeat this process with the cherry stone clams. Remove the clams from their shells, chop them coarsely, and reserve the broth in a separate container.

In the same pot, add the clarified butter, onions, celery, garlic and thyme. Sauté the mixture until the onions are translucent. Add flour to make a roux sauce, stirring pretty much constantly. Cook over a low heat for 5 minutes (don't brown). Slowly add the clam juice (fresh and commercial), stirring constantly to avoid lumps. Simmer for 10 minutes (the soup will be very thick at this point, so be careful it does not burn). Add the potatoes and cook until they are tender. Add the cream and clams and bring the pot back to the boil. Season to taste.

Note: 1 cup = 236.5ml/8oz
1 quart = 0.946l/2 pints

Published by Thomas Cook Publishing
Thomas Cook Holdings Ltd
PO Box 227
Thorpe Wood
Peterborough PE3 6PU
United Kingdom

Telephone: 01733 503571
Email: books@thomascook.com

Text © 2001 Thomas Cook Publishing
Maps © 2001 Thomas Cook Publishing

ISBN 1 841570 53 2

Distributed in the United States of
America by the Globe Pequot Press,
PO Box 480, Guilford, Connecticut
06437, USA

Publisher: Donald Greig
Commissioning Editor: Deborah Parker
Map Editor: Bernard Horton

Project management: Dial House
    Publishing
Series Editor: Christopher Catling
Copy Editor: Lucy Thomson
Proofreader: Jan Wiltshire

Series and cover design: WhiteLight
Cover artwork: WhiteLight and
    Kaarin Wall
Text layout: SJM Design Consultancy,
    Dial House Publishing
Maps prepared by Polly Senior
    Cartography

Repro and image setting: PDQ Digital
    Media Solutions Ltd
Printed and bound in Italy by
    Eurografica SpA

Written, researched and photographed by
Patricia Harris and **David Lyon**

We would like to thank the authors for the
photographs used in this book, to whom
the copyright belongs, with the exception
of the following:
Ethel Davis (page 56)
Caroline Jones (page 3).